CONTENTS

Introduction 4

Features of *Innovations* 6

Unit by unit notes 9

Unit 1a 9

Unit 1b 13

Unit 2a 16

Unit 2b 19

Review 1 and 2 23

Unit 3a 23

Unit 3b 28

Unit 4a 32

Unit 4b 37

Review 3 and 4 40

Unit 5a 41

Unit 5b 45

Unit 6a 50

Unit 6b 54

Review 5 and 6 58

Unit 7a 58

Unit 7b 64

Unit 8a 67

Unit 8b 71

Review 7 and 8 75

Unit 9a 76

Unit 9b 80

Unit 10a 84

Unit 10b 88

Review 9 and 10 92

INTRODUCTION

What's so innovative about *Innovations?*

Innovations sets out to maximise students' ability to speak English fluently and to be able to understand natural spoken English. It does this not simply by providing students with plenty of opportunities to use language in personal, creative and communicative contexts, but more importantly, it provides a predominantly spoken model of English.

The English presented in *Innovations* is the English commonly used in everyday life by fluent, educated speakers. The book's syllabus is designed to meet students' communicative needs. In every unit, the prime concern is with what students will be able to **say** afterwards. As a result, the driving force behind the structure of the book is not the atomistic tense-based structures of traditional grammar, but rather the typical kinds of conversations students want to be able to have in English.

What level is it for?

Innovations is for serious intermediate students keen to improve their spoken English, but also for upper-intermediate students who have studied a lot of English, but who are frustrated by their inability to put this knowledge into practice. This may seem different from many coursebooks, but it is an approach which reflects the realities of the classroom. Some intermediate students have the motivation which allows them to cope with slightly more demanding material, while some upper level students welcome the opportunity to study a course which consolidates what they already know and extends it.

Innovations helps these students see how words work in action with other words, and how conversation works in normal, everyday contexts. With its innovative syllabus and content based on the language of spoken English, it also avoids boring and limiting students by repeating the same few grammatical structures that they have already studied so many times before – and which they still cannot use effectively when speaking.

An innovation – but not a revolution!

While *Innovations* has deliberately re-prioritised the syllabus of the traditional intermediate coursebook, it does, nevertheless, contain all the tense-based grammar both students and teachers at this level expect to find. The difference is that these structures are presented and practised very much in contexts of everyday usage. Furthermore, because of the way in which the language in the book is presented, grammatical structures recur from unit to unit, always in meaningful contexts.

Innovations also has a broader concept of grammar than many other books. Grammar at both larger than and smaller than sentence level is also featured, and the book codifies and practises many of the features and patterns of spoken grammar that have previously been ignored by books which were more concerned with the grammar of the written language.

Getting students off the intermediate plateau

The real difference between intermediate students and advanced ones is not that the latter have a grasp of obscure, unusual grammatical structures, but rather that they have a far bigger, more flexible, and more developed vocabulary. They have many more phrases, collocations and fixed expressions, as well as individual words, available to them. In short, they can do a lot more with the English that they have.

To help get students off the intermediate plateau, *Innovations* provides a massive amount of lexis in all its shapes and forms. Much of this revolves around what have often been called conversational gambits – the language that oils the wheels of conversation, the kind of phrases and chunks of language that give students the ability to control conversations and to engage the people they are talking to. *Innovations* teaches students how to be vague in appropriate places, how to ask for clarification, how to express what they mean even when they lack the precise word or words, and so on. On top of this, *Innovations* also has a wealth of useful collocations, and extends students' ability to use the common verbs they have already encountered before. There are plenty of fixed and semi-fixed expressions too, as well as many useful individual words.

Notice the surrounding language

In the exercises, we have done our best to present language in natural contexts. This means that the surrounding language is just as important as the language being focused on. If the exercise is about the

INNOVATIONS
TEACHERS' BOOK

Hugh Dellar and Darryl Hocking

LTP

Language Teaching Publications

114a Church Rd, Hove, BN3 2EB, England

Tel: 00 44 (1) 273 736344

Fax: 00 44 (1) 273 775361

E-mail: ltp@ltpwebsite.com

ISBN   1 899396 26 8

© LTP 2000

Editors: Jimmie Hill, Michael Lewis, Morgan Lewis

Cover and overall design: Anna Macleod

Printed in England by Commercial Colour Press, London E7 0EW present perfect, do not miss the opportunity to point out common phrases and expressions at the same time. One of the most important ways students will improve on their own is if they notice more. Turn 'noticing' into a major classroom activity.

Organisation

Innovations is divided into ten two-part units. All the A units start with vocabulary and discussions or a short listening to help establish the topic. The main input is then a dialogue which is used first for listening comprehension and then for detailed listening for words and phrases. The dialogue forms the basis for many of the language exercises and activities which follow, as features of spoken English are highlighted and practised.

The B units start in a similar way, but the main input is a reading text with comprehension questions, vocabulary work and discussion of the topic. More lexical and functional activities follow.

The two sections of each unit are always related, either in very direct ways, as in Units 1 and 2, or in looser, more thematic ways, as in Unit 3, where the theme of flying in section B is presented in a text dealing with the kind of tough decisions focused on in section A. Similarly, 10b deals with work, a follow-on from the conversation presented in 10a.

If you are sharing a class with another teacher, one can use the A units while the other uses the B units. Each half unit provides around six hours of work.

Other components

A pack of two cassettes and a workbook complete this course. The cassettes contain all the presentation dialogues, pronunciation exercises and those lexical exercises where the stress and intonation are critical.

The workbook is for self-study, but any of the exercises may be done in class. In addition, the workbook contains writing tasks.

Some of the workbook exercises are directly related to activities in the students' book, making it useful for setting homework, while others are more loosely connected and are designed to extend students' knowledge. You may choose to use the workbook or you may decide that there is sufficient exercise material in the students' book. If you choose not to use the workbook as part of your course, it is a good idea to recommend it to students as follow-up study at the end of the course.

Finally

Innovations attempts to re-motivate students who have been studying for some years. It does this through its content, its approach, but also through its design. We hope that the use of colour to highlight useful language and the use of provocative photographs will help to stimulate your students and encourage them to make real progress.

Hugh Dellar and Darryl Hocking

FEATURES OF *INNOVATIONS*

The dialogues

The dialogues form the main input in each of the A sections. These are based on corpora of spoken English, but have been cleaned up to avoid the redundancy, overlapping and false starts common in everyday speech, while still retaining many other useful features of such speech. The dialogues are examples of typical conversations that people have about everyday topics, and contain many commonly-used phrases and expressions.

When using the dialogues in class, play the tape once for gist and then once more to allow students to identify the words and phrases which fill the gaps. If your class find this hard, play the tape a third time and pause after each gap to give students more time to write. Finally, play the tape one last time as students read the dialogue. Listening to natural spoken English like this whilst also reading what they are hearing helps students get used to the way language is chunked when we speak – realising where speakers pause, and more importantly, where they do not pause – and to notice other features of everyday speech.

You can get students to read the conversation aloud in pairs – either the whole dialogue or just part of it.

Much of the language presented and explored later in the units is drawn from the dialogues, so students get to see and hear this language in meaningful contexts first, before going on to practise it. For example, in the dialogue on page 10 Simon describes his brother as 'a bit old-fashioned, a bit traditional' and then in exercise 5 on page 11, students are presented with these and other modifiers.

The reading texts

These texts form the main input of the B units. The texts are derived from authentic articles, but have been re-written to include maximally useful vocabulary and collocations. The texts are all designed to elicit some kind of personal response from students, whether it be laughter, disbelief, or shock!

Encourage students to read the whole text through without worrying too much about any words they don't know – tell them to put their pens down for a minute and relax! Important vocabulary is focused on later, and students need to gain confidence in their ability to understand **most** – if not all – of a text. Encourage students to focus on the many words they

do know! It is important that students have the opportunity to react personally to the text. The Talking Points after the texts provide this opportunity.

The comprehension check questions often focus on particular lexical items within the text. Ask students how they chose their answers, which words in the text helped them decide. Students could also do this exercise in pairs first.

The Vocabulary check exercises are designed to encourage students to notice collocations within the text. Point out the way the words collocate and suggest that students record two-, three- and four-word collocations in their notebooks as well as individual words. Encourage students to use a good English-English dictionary, not just to check the meaning of words but also to read the examples given, which often contain useful collocations.

Extra reading texts

There are smaller texts, such as that found on page 14, in each unit, which are thematically linked to the broader topic. These fun, interesting articles are primarily designed to encourage discussion and lead into fluency work. They are followed by Talking Points, where students get the chance to discuss issues found in the texts. There are ideas on how to lead in to these texts in the notes on each unit, as well as advice on how to exploit the photos in class.

Although these texts are not especially intended for vocabulary work, they have also been re-written to include maximally useful, accessible vocabulary, and students' attention could be drawn to particular collocations within the texts.

Real English notes

There are notes on real English throughout the book – phrases, words and grammatical features commonly used in everyday English, but overlooked by many more traditional coursebooks and grammars. There are both explanations and examples given in these notes, and you can simply point them out to students as little extras or add more examples of your own.

The Review Units at the end of every two units recycle much of the language highlighted in the Real English sections, and re-present it in other common contexts.

Talking Points

There are Talking Points throughout the book. These are intended both as a way of encouraging students to use some of the new language that they have met, in personalised ways, and also as an opportunity for students to relax and enjoy talking to each other! You may wish to use these discussion periods as a chance to monitor students' spoken performance and to gather student errors to focus on later, or as a chance to listen out for gaps in students' vocabularies which can later be addressed, or simply as a chance for you to move around the class, enjoy your students' company and share your own thoughts and experiences. However, always bear in mind that students are entitled not to join in discussions which make them feel uncomfortable.

Vocabulary Pages

Each B unit is followed by a Vocabulary page. These pages develop and extend the vocabulary areas focused on in each unit and can either be given as homework or done in class. If you use them in class, they can be done individually or in pairs and then checked in the whole class.

When going through this section, it is important to point out features of lexis to students. For example, you could draw students' attention to the way in which common verbs have lots of useful collocations commonly used with them. For example, *watch, see, look* on page 55. Encourage students to keep records of any new collocations for such verbs that they meet. Similarly, you might want to mention the fixed nature of the vast majority of idioms and expressions – and see if similar expressions exist in the students' first language. If students do want to translate new words, always encourage them to record **whole expressions** or collocations, rather than individual words.

Learning Advice

Learning advice pages occur throughout the book. See page 22 for an example. They are primarily there to give the students useful hints about how best to approach their learning, but you could use them as the basis of class discussions on learning styles, keeping vocabulary records, accents and so on. It is useful for students to have the methodology and thinking behind the materials and the teaching made explicit.

Jokes

There are jokes in most units, partly to bring some light relief and extra humour into the class, and partly because being able to tell jokes is an important part of daily life. Students practise telling jokes, and focus on the pausing, stress and intonation that make a good joke-teller.

Review units

There is a Review every two units. This gives students the chance to revisit and consolidate language they have studied. These units can be done as homework or as tests in class time. The final section, however, the Vocabulary Quiz, is best done in pairs or groups or even with the whole class divided into two teams. You could even award points and score it as if it was a real TV quiz show!

Pronunciation

As *Innovations* places such an emphasis on spoken English, pronunciation is given a high priority throughout. The tape provides models of many short dialogues, language patterns and expressions. The tape can be used to help students practise the expressions. They should be encouraged to repeat the expressions several times chorally and individually until they can say them naturally. It is important that students do not just learn forms and meanings, but also learn how whole phrases and expressions are said by fluent speakers.

The Tapescript

The Tapescript starts on page 166 and features all of the dialogues with the missing words and phrases highlighted in red for easier identification. As well as the dialogues and listenings, many of the language practice activities are also on tape.

The Grammar Commentary

The Grammar Commentary starts on page 176. It begins with two pages outlining the basic approach to grammar taken in the book. Ask students to read these pages early on in the course, and make time to answer any questions they may have. The 40 grammar points that follow are all cross-referenced to exercises within the units. For example, at the top of exercise 10 on page 76, you see G18, which refers to Grammar point 18 on page 182. Students can be asked to read the grammar commentary either before or after trying the exercises in each unit. The commentary combines explanation with useful examples, which help students to see how grammar is actually used in everyday language.

The photographs

Photographs play an important role throughout the book, and many exercises ask students very specifically to describe photos (page 15, for example), to role play situations depicted in them (see page 19 for an example), to respond personally to them (pages 112-113) and so on. Ideas about how to use photos like this are generally mentioned in the rubrics, and additional ideas are also given in individual unit notes in this book.

However, as *Innovations* is so rich in interesting visuals, the book can also be treated as a photo resource library and pictures can be used to do activities not directly related to the coursebook. For example, you may be working through Unit 4b, but there is nothing to stop you using the photo on page 136 to set up a role play between a traffic warden and a driver in your afternoon class, or to use the wedding photo on page 126 to set up a debate on getting married or just living together.

The language strips as a resource

The language strips at the beginning of both Part A and Part B of each unit provide valuable input which can be exploited in many different ways. They are particularly useful as a source of 5-minute filler activities, between more substantial activities or at the end of a lesson. You should not, however, try to go through all the language in any strip. Instead, try to ensure students notice and learn two or three expressions from each strip.

The language of the strips

All the expressions are correct, natural, usually spoken language, including a combination of idioms, fixed expressions and expressions containing phrasal verbs. Often there are also some more colloquial topic-specific expressions and occasionally one or two more jokey expressions connected to something mentioned in the unit. The language of the strips is useful for all students, but particularly those who have had less chance to use their English in 'real' situations. Encourage students to notice that many of the expressions, usually those which contain the word 'I', are useful in talking about yourself, your opinions and reactions.

Some of the expressions contain one less common word, for example: *The sort of things you get a kick out of* (2a). Almost always these are idioms, common in the spoken language. For these, students should look up the phrases **at the end** of the dictionary entry for the unknown word, in this case, *kick*.

If all the words in an expression are common, explain to students that they must notice and learn the whole phrase exactly as it appears in *Innovations*. If they translate expressions from the strips, they need to find an equivalent in their own language, not a word-for-word translation.

Using the strips

Students can look at the strips alone but they are probably best used for pair or small-group activities in class. Here are a number of activities which can be used for most of the strips.

1. Ask students to find the expressions:

a. which are responses to two or three questions or remarks you write on the board

b. which express very neatly a complicated idea you express in a roundabout way, for example, in 4b, *It's too early to go home. There is so much more we can do. (The night is young.)*

2. Copy some of the expressions onto an overhead transparency, leaving some gaps. Ask students to complete the expressions before opening their books, then compare their answers with the strip.

3. Pairs or groups identify expressions which:

a. contain a familiar idiom

b. contain expressions with a phrasal verb

c. are very colloquial

d. contain language which has occurred in an earlier unit, such as modifiers or softeners: *a bit of a, just* etc

4. Pairs or groups sort the expressions according to some 'rule' such as :

a. positive *v* negative expressions

b. formal *v* informal expressions

c. those which are more likely to be used by men/women

d. those more likely to be used by young/older people

e. remarks which initiate a conversation *v* responses

5. Perhaps the most important groups into which learners can sort the language is expressions they would like to use themselves *v* expressions they would not feel comfortable using.

When students identify expressions they would like to use themselves, encourage them to add them to the Expression Organiser on pages 187-191 of the Students' Book.

Throughout *Innovations* the pictures and language strips provide ways of introducing the topic and some of the language relevant to the unit.

UNIT BY UNIT NOTES

Unit 1a
Talking about people

Unit Overview

Topic

Describing friends and family and talking about what they do.

The dialogue

Melanie and Simon talk about their families.

Language input

- Modifiers – *really nice, quite young, a bit boring*
- Present tenses – simple and continuous and collocations with *work, run* and *do*
- Adjectives – describing people's character and appearance
- Softening expressions – *Well, actually, To be honest,* etc

Reading text

The Pridham family – 19 children!

The language strip

Here are some questions you can use with the class to exploit the language in the language strip.

> Which of the expressions are about a person's appearance and which are about their personality?
> Which of the expressions contain idioms?
> Which contain phrasal verbs?

Encourage students to add some of the expressions from the language strip to the Expression Organiser on page 187.

1 Describing people

You may want to use the photos on page 8 to elicit descriptions before doing the task with the vocabulary list. Model the task for the students by choosing three of your friends or family and then choosing the best expressions to describe them. Teachers modelling tasks like this for students can help to provide a very useful source of input – and, of course, it helps humanise you too!

If students need help using the vocabulary in full expressions, spend a few minutes checking students are aware of how to **use** the words in context, for example: *He's got fair / dark / completely white hair; He's*

going grey; He's losing his hair; He's almost bald. Students don't just need to know the meaning of a word, they also need to have their attention drawn to how words work in phrases and how they're typically used.

Workbook

Give exercise 14, page 12 for homework.

2 Who's who? (T1)

You could ask students to describe the people in the pictures before they hear the tape. Allow the students to hear the tape more than once if necessary.

Answers

1 is Nick; 2 is Kirsty; 3 is Matt; 4 is Jenny.

Photo opportunity

Ask students to discuss if any of the people pictured on page 8 remind them of anyone they know or have met and in what way. Feed in language to help them, such as *This girl looks a bit like a German friend of mine* and *This man reminds me a bit of my grandad.*

Alternatively, ask students to guess how old each person is and what they do. Feed in useful structures if needed. For example: *The man with the moustache looks about 35; This girl must be in her early twenties; She might be a fashion student or something like that.*

Ask students to discuss whether or not they've ever – or **would** ever – dress like the people in the pictures or have their hair like that. Ask the class to discuss why/why not, and to give extra details where possible.

All three of the activities above could also be used with the four pictures on page 9.

3 While you listen (T2)

Set the scene. Check students know what 'popped in to Melanie's house' means. Make use of the Real English note on *the brother from hell* at this point if you wish.

Tell the class not to try to understand every word but only try to answer the two questions. We suggest the text is covered the first time you play the tape. Play the tape twice if necessary so that students can answer the questions. Check their answers.

Answers

1. Melanie's an only child, Simon's got an older brother and a younger sister.
2. Melanie gets on well with her mum, but she doesn't really get on with her dad.
   Simon gets on well with his sister, but not so well with his brother.

Now see if they can fill in the first two or three gaps from memory with a partner. Play the tape again for students to fill in the missing words. Pause the tape so they have time to write in what they hear. Finally, play the tape again with students listening while reading the tapescript on page 166. The missing words are highlighted in red. You may want students to read the dialogue, or part of it, in pairs.

Don't be afraid to ask students to listen several times. The more students listen to natural spoken English, the more chance they have of acquiring that language and improving their own performance.

4 Talking Point

These discussion points can be done as a class or in small groups and can take as little or as much time as you like.

5 Modifiers (T3) (G1)

Let students compare their answers for 1-5 and ask them to say a bit more about the people they have described. Again, you could model some of these if you want to. You might also want to work on any adjectives that you feel are being used wrongly.

Answers

The examples of modifiers in the conversation between Simon and Melanie are:

they're both really busy/they sound really interesting/I find my dad a bit dull/he's quite nice/she's really nice/a bit too nice, though, sometimes/She's a bit over-protective/a bit old-fashioned, a bit traditional/he's a bit, how can I put it, right-wing/He's a bit of a fool

Workbook

4 Expressions with prepositions, page 9
17 Absolutely, page 13

6 Pronunciation (T4)

Point out the additional context in which these sentences would be said, which helps to make the meanings clear. for example:
If we say *I live **quite** near the office*, we might then add

but not near enough to walk or anything. However, if we say *I live quite **near** the office*, we'd probably then add something like *which means I can walk in to work*. Ask students what they think might be said next after each version of 2-8.

7 Talking Points

All these sentences contain modifiers. Encourage students to share their opinions in small groups before getting a class consensus. This is a great chance for the class to let off a bit of steam! Try to remain impartial yourself!

Photo opportunity

Ask the class to describe what they can see in the pictures here. Feed in relevant vocabulary, such as *They've got ripped jeans on, They've got a tear in the back of their jeans, She's got tattoos all over her hand*. Make sure you give the class **whole phrases**, not just isolated words such as *pierced*.

The pictures can then be used to encourage debate on why people feel the need to have piercings and tattoos, whether they suit some people or not, whether anyone in the class has, or would have, any done, etc.

Alternatively, students could prepare a role play between a teenager who wants to get their face pierced and a tattoo on their arm, and a concerned parent. Divide the class into two groups – a parent group and a teenager group – and give them five minutes to plan what they are going to say, what line of argument they are going to follow. Feed in vocabulary where necessary. Brainstorm a list of useful phrases beforehand to give each group, if possible. For example:

All my friends have got them.
I can always take it out if I get sick of it.
It might go septic.
You'll be stuck with it for life.

You could also prepare a list on a handout or transparency of twenty possible things that might be said between parent and child in a conversation like that above, and ask the class to decide which were said by the parent and which by the teenager.

8 Present tenses

As well as introducing present tenses, this activity draws students' attention to some typical patterns for talking about what people do. Write *I'm ... I work ... I run ... I do ...* on the board and ask students to read about Audrey and Andy and complete the sentences with the information they find. Point out the four patterns highlighted in the box. Then do the exercise.

Answers

1. 'm 2. works 3. 's 4. work 5. works 6. work 7. 's
8. 's 9. 's 10. do 11. does 12. 's 13. work 14. runs

Extension activity: divide the class into two groups and ask them to list a typical day in the life of one of the two characters. For example:

I get up at around six, so I can catch all the people trying to get to work.
I usually stop for a coffee at around 11, once the rush hour is over.

This gives you a chance to see how well they already use the present simple.

Alternatively, put students in pairs and ask them to discuss who they think has a better life-style, Audrey or Andy, and why.

Talking Point

Students may need help with vocabulary when trying to describe what their parents do. Tell students not to worry if they can't say exactly what the jobs are. This is a good chance to introduce structures like this:

He's a kind of businessman or something.
She runs some kind of import-export business.

A further activity is to brainstorm a list of jobs that the class think are potentially embarrassing and ask them to rank them in order of social unacceptability!

Workbook

6 Jobs 1 – collocations, page 9

Grammar discussion (G2)

The A-sentences all talk or ask about things the speaker sees as permanent, timeless facts, while the B-sentences are all seen as being temporary, relating to particular periods of time.

Present continuous time expressions:

this month | at the moment | this weekend | again | at the moment

Make sure you draw students' attention to the fact that the present continuous is used with time expressions that make the temporary nature of the event described clear – *this month, at the moment*, and so on. The absence of time expressions for the present simple is because the events described are seen as generalisations.

Grammar in context

Ask students to compare and discuss their answers in pairs, and then ask the whole class how they made

their decisions and which other words helped them decide on the tense.

Answers

1. works, 's working, 's trying
2. 's acting, 's not normally (or *isn't normally*)
3. runs, 's looking after
4. don't talk, Don't you get on
5. 's, 's still waiting
6. aren't talking, 's still

Students might want to compare their answers for 7-9 and to chat about these.

Famous present tenses

This is optional. Use as much or as little of this activity as you want. You may want to use number 2 to ask students what their impression of English or British people is.

Answers

What goes up must come down is used in situations where you want to say that one thing inevitably follows another. For example, if someone is very annoyed, you know they will calm down eventually.

You use *An elephant never forgets* when you remember something that someone said or did to you that they would prefer you to forget.

You would say *It never rains, but it pours* when something bad has just happened to you – just after two or three other bad things have also happened.

If you tell someone *They're making a mountain out of a molehill*, you mean they're worrying too much about something that is really a very small problem.

Workbook

Use the exercises on page 8 in class or for homework to consolidate work on present tenses.

9 Adjectives

It is important that you stress the subjective nature of these – and, indeed, most – adjectives describing personality. There are no correct P/N answers here, though obviously certain words, like *messy*, are more commonly used negatively, while others, like *sensible*, are generally positive.

Ask students to explain why the words have positive or negative connotations for them.

Stress

re<u>li</u>gious tra<u>di</u>tional <u>qui</u>et <u>tal</u>kative
<u>ti</u>dy laid-<u>back</u> con<u>ser</u>vative am<u>bi</u>tious
business-<u>min</u>ded (or <u>busi</u>ness-minded)
indi<u>vi</u>dual <u>mess</u>y <u>li</u>beral hard-<u>wor</u>king <u>sen</u>sible

Judging by appearances

If students lack ideas, give them a few extra words on the board to use. Encourage them to use *a bit, quite, really* etc.

Workbook

9 Keep, page 10
15 Describing people, page 12

10 Full-time job

Lead in to the text by asking the class who comes from the biggest family, how many children is **too** many, how many kids they would like to end up having themselves, and why. Tell the class they are going to read a text about a family bigger than any of theirs – the Pridham family from England. Ask them to guess how large the family is, and then let them read the text. This text is here purely to amuse and even shock. You may want to ask a couple of comprehension questions, such as *What do the Pridhams do for a living?* and *How are they going to deal with the problem of clothing all their children?*

The Talking Point in exercise 10 gives students the opportunity to discuss their personal reactions to the text.

11 How much / many?

This is a way of practising the grammar of *much* and *many*, which students at this level have often done many times before, but disguised as a fun, interactive, chatty exercise. All the questions are *how much* questions. When students have finished discussing their answers in pairs, ask them to change questions 2, 3 and 6 into *how many* questions: *How many loaves of bread do you ...? How many packets of breakfast cereal do you ...? How many newspapers do you buy a week?* etc. There is more on *much* and *many* on page 33 and page 179 in the Grammar Commentary.

12 Emphasising (T5)

This activity encourages students to describe things more fluently by repeating adverbs and using synonyms. Remember students may need to listen and repeat several times. Encourage students to say things such as:

Her shoes were really great, really way out.

Photo opportunity

A fun way of extending the task is to ask students to think of things that the objects themselves might say, using two adjectives and the same adverb. For example, the shoe might say *Oh no, look at her feet.*

They look really big and really smelly! while the bear might say *Oh, this water is really nice, really warm* or *How would you feel if I watched you having a bath?*

13 Softening

If students find it difficult to work out what might have been said for 1-6, give them these prompts for the first two:

1. dad / job?
2. What / think / food?

Then go round and help with 3-6 as necessary.

Possible answers

1. So does your dad like his job?
2. So what did you think of the food there?
3. I don't want to go round to their house tonight, but if you really want to ...
4. Would you like to come round and see my model aeroplane collection later?
5. How do you feel about going to watch a baseball match? Would you like to?
6. I was wondering if maybe you wanted to come to Stephen's party with me?

The new girlfriend

This activity is an entertaining way to get students practising the softening language just presented. Make sure students are aware of this, and encourage them to use the three softening expressions as much as possible.

It's useful for students to do activities like this again a day or two – or even a week – later. You could ask students to re-try the task the following lesson, but with the three expressions covered up to see how well they remember them.

Workbook

13 Softening your message, page 11 extends the idea of softening what you say.

Photo opportunity

This picture could be used in combination with the photos on page 11 to help spark debate on the topic of body piercing. You could also use it to lead in to a discussion on changing times. Students brainstorm trends and fashions for women and/or men over the last ten or twenty years, and then discuss which they prefer and why. Feed in relevant phrases and collocations to help the students out. A more advanced class could discuss why people choose to make themselves look like this, if such appearances are purely personal or if they have a deeper significance, and so on.

Expression Organiser

Don't forget to introduce students to the Expression Organiser on page 187.

Read the short introduction at the top of the page and ask the students to translate the expressions into their own language for homework or with a student with the same mother tongue. Emphasise how it is vital to translate the expression as a whole, not word-for-word. Tell them to spend time at home reading through the unit again and adding any other expressions they want to be able to use themselves.

Unit 1b
Friends and relatives

Unit Overview

Topic

More about family and friends

The text

A criminal's son meets his father as an adult for the first time.

Language input

- Giving bad news – *Oh, haven't you heard?*
- Vocabulary for people you know – *partner, godson*
- Comparatives – *quite a lot better*
- Telling a joke

Vocabulary page

The language strip

Ask one or more of these questions to introduce and exploit the language in the strip:

Which expressions are negative?
Can you find expressions which suggest:

  a. *You have a really good relationship with someone*
  b. *You don't really like someone*
  c. *Someone needs to work harder*
  d. *Someone has died*

Lead in

To lead in to the theme of the text, ask students if they have ever met up with any distant relatives that they hadn't seen for ages. When? Where? What was it like? Have they got any other relatives that they have never met? Where?

1 Collocations

You can either give the answers if students don't know them or come back to this exercise after the text has been read.

Answers

1. up 2. sentence 3. touch

2 While reading

You might want the class to speculate on the answer to question 1 briefly before reading the text. Remind students that they do not need to understand every word to answer the questions. Encourage students to answer the questions in their own words. They do not have to quote whole chunks of the text.

Answers

1. He was originally sentenced for robbery and burglary, but his original sentence has been extended because he keeps attacking other prisoners and taking them hostage.
2. Never – although according to the text, Michael was three when his father went to prison, so in some sense they had 'met'.
3. He's planning to open up a restaurant with his son and to be the security on the door.

3 Comprehension check

Give students five minutes to decide on their own answers and compare in pairs before you check the answers. Ask why they think the statements are true or false, as this involves referring back to key lexis within the text.

Answers

1. False – it's his dad who's the most dangerous man.
2. False – he's unbelievably strong.
3. False – he was shocked to hear about it.
4. True – he said it was very nice to meet him.
5. False – his father's got a large, bushy beard.
6. True – they want to run their own restaurant.

4 Vocabulary check

Tell students the relevant paragraph numbers if you want to speed up this activity.

Answers

1. reunited (paragraph 1) 2. burglary (paragraph 2)
3. hostage, hostages (paragraph 2) 4. infamous (paragraph 3) 5. hug (paragraph 4) 6. bushy (paragraph 4)

Workbook

10 Re- verbs, page 10 (reconsider, remarry etc)

5 Talking Point

The first part of this Talking Point can be developed into a role play between Michael and his wife if you wish.

The second part about the pros and cons of prison can develop into a bigger classroom debate with students working in pairs and then fours and then ending up with a whole class discussion. If so, spend time brainstorming and supplying some useful vocabulary, such as:

rehabilitate criminals, reintegrate back into society, do community service, pay a heavy fine, petty crime, serious crime, alternative methods of punishment,

persistent re-offenders, It's a waste of time and money, It just doesn't work.

You could prepare and distribute a list of phrases like this and give students five minutes to prepare their arguments before the discussion begins.

See the **Workbook** (page 13) for a written task on the same subject.

6 Giving bad news (T6)

There are two ways of doing this activity. Students can match up the dialogues first, then check their answers by listening to the tape. Alternatively, they cover the responses a-h and read 1-8 only. They then listen to the taped conversations. After that, they look at the responses a-h and match them up. Then, they listen again to confirm their answers. This has the advantage of students listening to the same thing twice. If you want students to read the dialogues in pairs, it is easier if you use the tapescript on page 166.

Answers

1e 2c 3f 4a 5h 6g 7b 8d

The expressions used to introduce bad news are:
a. I'm afraid not.
b. Well, actually, ...
c. I don't know how to put this, but ...
d. Unfortunately, I'm afraid ...
e. I'm sorry, I'm afraid I can't.
f. Well, actually, ...
g. Well, actually, ...
h. Well, yes, I'm afraid ...

7 Role play

You may want to brainstorm or give students relevant language that these photos suggest to help with the role plays. For example:

balanced on the edge of a cliff | everybody's been evacuated | It happened so suddenly | It's a disaster | gone up in flames | spread very quickly | put it out | turned upside down | smashed to pieces | Nobody's hurt.

Ask pairs of students to choose one of the situations to create a short phone call. Give a few minutes' preparation time before students try the conversations. Ask them to repeat the conversations once or even twice more. Explain that repeating exactly the same thing improves their performance. You might want to give them the homework task of trying to memorise the words and expressions so they can use them to repeat the task again in the next lesson.

8 Talking Point

Before reading this update on Charles Bronson, remind the class that Bronson intended to start a new life in business with his son. Ask the class to vote on whether they think this has happened or not, then read the text aloud to the class as they just listen or listen and read. Discuss the questions under the text in groups or as a class. The discussion could be extended by asking the class if they have read any books about criminals or if they enjoy watching films about criminals. Why are such books and films so popular?

When students are underlining new expressions, encourage them to notice collocations, and to underline not just new words on their own, but the other words which collocate with them, such as:

prison authorities, seems increasingly unlikely, caused over (half a million) pounds' worth of damage.

9 Friends and relatives

When discussing whether students have similar sayings in their own language, you could also ask the class if these four aphorisms are true.

This exercise is also another good chance for you to model the task by talking about a few people in your life that fit these descriptions. You could also try and recycle some of the language from the unit as you do so. It is very important for students to hear this kind of controlled, recycling teacher-talk.

10 Comparatives (G3)

Answers

1. stronger
2. better
3. cheaper
4. older, wiser
5. younger

Talk about yourself

Make sure students realise they have to add real names here, as well as adverbs or adverb phrases. Encourage students to give true examples of people in their lives. Language is much easier to learn if it's connected to something in our own lives. Students should come to feel that they somehow **own** this new language.

Workbook

8 The more . . . , the more . . . , page 10

11 An interesting friend

Give students a few minutes to prepare what they want to say. This is a good chance for students to mingle and talk to a few different people. The act of telling and retelling will help develop both accuracy and fluency.

12 A family joke (T7)

Play the tape or read the joke yourself if you prefer, but if you use the tape, pause immediately after *when I took her home,* and in pairs, ask students to tell each other how they think the joke ends. Then play the whole joke again without pausing so the punchline comes with full effect. Once students have listened to the joke, use the tape to draw their attention to where the speaker pauses and, just as importantly, where he doesn't pause. Then get students practising telling the joke themselves in pairs. You could then ask them if they can think of any other family-related jokes.

The punchline is: *The only trouble was when I took her home, my dad didn't like her.*

Vocabulary Page

The vocabulary page can be used as either homework or classwork.

Running and doing

1. do 2. run 3. run 4. do 5. run 6. do 7. runs 8. do 9. run 10. run

Types of people

1. laugh 2. bore 3. snobs 4. loner 5. show-off 6. weirdo

Idioms

1. legs 2. leg 3. neck 4. foot 5. head 6. face 7. chest 8. eyes

1. eye 2. moment 3. close 4. wavelength

Phrasal verbs with *up*

1. get 2. pick 3. Cheer 4. look 5. fill 6. mix

Extra workbook exercises

5   Phrasal verbs with *with*, page 9
7   Jobs 2 – expressions, page 9
11 Expressions with *make / do*, page 11
12 *Make* and *do* in context, page 11
16 Crime, page 12
18 Writing, page 13

Unit 2a
Your interests

Unit Overview

Topic

Talking about the things that interest you.

The dialogue

Dan and Helena have just started going out together and are trying to decide how to spend an evening.

Language input

- Using *thing* – *Jazz and blues and things like that*
- Agreeing – *So do I, Neither do I, Me too* etc
- Expressing dislike – *It's not really my kind of thing.*
- The *-ing* form – *I spend a lot of time windsurfing.*
- Time expressions – *once or twice a month, hardly ever* etc
- Listening for useful expressions

Reading text

Designer carrier bags

Learning advice

Ask students to read page 22, then discuss it in pairs. Then ask two pairs to work together and then finally discuss the relative importance of grammar and vocabulary as a whole class.

These learning advice pages come throughout the book and provide opportunities to discuss course content, learning styles, and similar issues. You can use them at any time, but do try to incorporate them into the course.

The language strip

Ask these questions to introduce and exploit some of the language in the strip:

Which expressions include either 'sort of' or 'kind of'? How would you say those expressions in your own language?

1 Free time

This is best done in pairs. Students may find that *often, sometimes* and *never* do not express accurately enough how often they do these things so give them some more adverbs and expressions as they ask for them. More expressions will be presented later on page 27 and 29. You may also want to introduce the expressions *We've got a lot in common / We don't have much in common.*

Photo opportunity

In pairs, students list as many verb + noun collocations as they can think of that are connected to these three pictures. Whichever pair has the most acceptable collocations wins. Encourage students to think about collocations such as *get a drink, stick to water, pick up a real bargain.* Alternatively, ask students to act out or write out a conversation which could happen in one of these places, maybe between two people in the club, or a person joining the gym and the instructor, or between a shopper and shop-owner in the junk shop.

2 Before you listen (T8)

Make sure students know what 'going out together' means in this context – that they are girlfriend and boyfriend. People often ask couples the question *So how long have you been going out together?*

Without reading the dialogue, students listen and decide which statement 1, 2 or 3 is most accurate.

Answer

They have less in common than they think.

Then let them read the dialogue as you play the tape again. Then, in pairs, ask the students to fill in the first two or three gaps from memory, then play the tape with pauses so that they can check and fill in the missing words. Do this two or three gaps at a time until the end. Play the tape through one more time with students following the script. Listening to the same language again and again is vital for students who want to improve their spoken English.

You may want students to read the dialogue, or parts of it, in pairs.

Workbook

1 Go and ... , page 14

3 Talking Point

'At what age are you too old to go clubbing?' This is a fun discussion to follow the intensive listening activity.

Photo opportunity

An opportunity to recycle some of the adjectives and structures from Unit 1. Ask students to describe the couple here, and to make guesses about where they are, where they are going, what they do, etc. They will need to use the following structures:

They look ...
They look like ...
They look as if they're ...

4 Pronunciation (T9)

Students need to get used to the fact that words are frequently linked in speech. Illustrate this with *kind of*. It is written as two separate words, but is said as a single unit. Get students to say the examples on the tape several times, both chorally and individually.

5 Three uses of *thing* (T10)

A nice way of introducing or rounding up this activity might be to let students ask you these 5 questions, and to give your own personal answers using the structures in 2 and 3.

6 Agreeing (G4)

Students will be pleased to learn that *Me too / Me neither* can be used with any auxiliary verbs. Make sure students realise there are **two** correct responses in the Grammar in context exercise and they must cross out the wrong one.

Answers

Grammar in context
The incorrect responses are:
1. So have I. 2. Me too. 3. Neither do I. 4. Neither have I. 5. So do I. 6. Me neither.

Auxiliary verb practice
1. So do I. 2. Neither do I. 3. So am I. 4. So have I. 5. Neither do I. 6. So would I. 7. So was I. 8. Neither can I.

Workbook

2 So (do) I / Neither (do) I, page 14

7 Not really keen (T11)

This activity follows on naturally from the previous activity. Write on the board: *I really love classical music and opera*. Ask the class to agree (*So do I, Me too*). Now ask them how they would respond if they **don't** like classical music and opera. Respond to their ideas and then show them the conversations in the blue box. After students have matched the two-line conversations, play the tape with the class following the tapescript on page 167. Then get them to read the dialogues in pairs.

Answers

1b 2f 3a 4e 5d 6c

The examples of *really* in this exercise are:
a. it's not really my kind of thing/I don't really understand.
b. Really? I'm not really very keen on them myself.
c. It's not really my kind of thing.

d. I don't really like things like that myself.
e. I'm not really that keen on ...
f. It's not really my kind of thing.

Collocations
1. winter sports 2. have fun 3. interested in politics 4. It's not my kind of thing. 5. get hurt 6. classical music 7. I don't see the point of it. 8. It put me off for life.

8 I really love it

The activities are: golf, snorkelling, cycling, tennis, football, surfing/windsurfing, diving.

As students are telling each other whether they like doing these things or not, encourage them to use the language from the two previous activities. For example:

I'm not really very keen on golf myself.
> No, me neither. It looks really boring, doesn't it?

Make sure students know not just the nouns shown here, but the whole phrases we use to describe these activities – *play golf, go snorkelling, go cycling* (if it's just as a hobby) / *cycling* (if it's more serious and competitive), *play tennis, play football, go windsurfing, go surfing*, and *diving*.

Depending on the interests of your students, you may want to extend the vocabulary work on one or two of these sports (there is a vocabulary exercise on football and tennis in the Workbook, page 15).

The final task under the pictures is best done with all the students in class walking about and mingling. Again, encourage genuine responses.

9 The *-ing* form (G5)

Remember there is a General Introduction to the grammar in *Innovations* on page 176/7 and detailed notes for individual grammar points in the Grammar Commentary on pages 178-186. This exercise is a good opportunity to introduce these two reference sections to the class.

The *-ing* form as a verb

Answers

Pattern 1: whenever I can/as often as I can/quite often/on Tuesdays
Pattern 2: most of my evenings/all my Saturday mornings/all my life/half my life

When students are discussing which of the things in the blue box they enjoy doing, it gives them the chance to re-use some of the language from exercises 6 and 7.

Answers

1. surfing the net
2. studying English/Spanish/Russian, etc
3. raising money for sick animals
4. singing
5. gardening/visiting gardens
6. planning my summer holidays
7. mountaineering/hill-walking
8. helping homeless people

The -*ing* form as a noun

Although the focus here is on grammar, it's fun to let students argue about the ideas they have. Numbers 1, 2, 5, 6 and 8 in particular can cause fairly heated debate in the right class – and much laughter!

Possible answers

1. Ballroom dancing 2. mountaineering
3. Sailing 4. Going off travelling 5. Learning Japanese 6. Helping the poor/homeless/elderly
7. Learning to ride a motorbike 8. Visiting gardens

Workbook

6 -*ing* forms, page 16
12 Need + -*ing*, page 18
14 -*ing* forms, page 19 (used with 13 Paragraph ordering, page 18)

Photo opportunity

This picture (page 28) can be used to get a discussion going about brand name products. Ask students to make a list of what they think are the six most famous brands in their country and then to compare their lists with a partner. In pairs, they should now agree on a new Top 10. In groups of four, students then discuss how each brand is different, what kind of image they project, what defines the brand, how they advertise their products and so on. You could bring in advertisements and ask students to analyse what techniques the companies are using to try and sell their brands. Students could also discuss their own feelings towards brand name products.

10 Are you a bag person?

This text is mainly for stimulating light-hearted discussion, so encourage students not to worry about any new words, but if they insist, remember to focus on whole chunks or collocations, not individual words.

One way to lead into this text is to find if people in the class collect things. Ask questions such as:

What do you collect? How many have you got?

You could ask if anyone is wearing anything with a designer label. Was it bought because it has the label or is it really better quality?

Alternatively, you could just jump straight in by telling students they're going to read a text about a fairly weird kind of interest – collecting carrier bags!

Students might also like to know that homeless women who live out of plastic bags are sometimes called 'bag ladies'.

11 Time expressions

Note that even though *I guess* is supposedly American English, it is very common in British English as an alternative to *I suppose.*

Once students have ranked the expressions according to frequency, ask students to repeat the expressions several times, making sure they can say them as natural whole phrases.

Answers

1. every day 2. every other day 3. two or three times a week 4. almost every weekend 5. every fortnight 6. once or twice a month 7. every month or so 8. a couple of times a year 9. hardly ever 10. never

12 How often do you . . . ?

You might want to start or finish this activity by letting the class ask you a few of these questions, and answer by first using one of the expressions from exercise 11 and then adding a bit of extra information. For example:

So how often do you have your hair cut?
> Oh, every month or so. It depends. I have it cut more in the summer, because I like my hair longer in the winter.

A variation on this task is to ask students to first write down how they **think** their partner will answer each question, and then to check by asking.

13 Not as often as I used to (T12)

Answers

1. often 2. time 3. often 4. every
5. Whenever 6. couple 7. ever 8. used

After students have listened to and completed these expressions, ask them to repeat them several times. Then get them to think of something they don't do as much as they'd like to or as often as they should. See the Workbook, page 17, for a related exercise.

Photo opportunity

You might want to ask students if it is common to have women bus drivers where they come from. If not, why not? What about women lorry drivers, or women pilots?

Alternatively, ask students to talk about any bus journeys they regularly make, how they feel about travelling by bus, if they ever chat to people on buses, anything strange or funny or unusual that's ever happened to them on a bus, how they'd feel about actually being a bus driver, etc.

14 Talking Point

Choose one or two of these for discussion in small groups or as a class.

Any of these questions could be turned into a simple written homework assignment, either instead of class discussion or as follow-up to the discussion.

Unit 2b
Unusual interests

Unit Overview

Topic

The subject is still interests and free-time activities but considers women doing sports traditionally done only by men, as well as popular leisure activities which can be very dangerous.

Reading text

This article considers the case of a woman boxer who wants women boxers to be given official status.

Language input

- *How*-questions – *How long did it take? How well can you speak it?* etc
- How much / how many
- Used to – *I used to play volleyball when I was younger.*
- Expressions with *would* and *'d* – *I would if I could, That'd be great* etc
- Checking you understand – *What? Do you mean watching it or actually playing it?*

Reading text

Scottish Kickboxers

Vocabulary Page

The language strip

Ask students to find four questions. Ask them what might be said to prompt those questions. What would make you say *Not in a month of Sundays?* or *It should be banned?*

Remind students to add some of the expressions that they want to use themselves to the Expression Organiser on page 187.

1 An unusual interest

Use the photo on page 31 to introduce the topic of women boxing. Ask a couple of questions:

What do you think of women boxing?
Do you see it in the same way as men boxing?

Introduce the text – Jane Couch, a women's boxing champion, is having a problem with the British Boxing Board of Control (BBBC). Ask the class to speculate on what the arguments are against women boxing before they read the text to find out.

Answer

The arguments against women boxing put forward by the BBBC are that women are biologically and emotionally unstable.

2 Help with words

If you feel it is necessary, you could point out the vocabulary before they read the text.

3 Comprehension check

Give students five minutes to decide on their own answers. Then ask them to compare answers in pairs before you check their answers. Ask why they think the statements are true or false, as this encourages students to refer to key lexis in the text.

Answers

1. False – it stands for the British Boxing Board of Control.
2. True.
3. False – that's the sum she could expect to earn if she could box officially.
4. False – she's mocking the BBBC's arguments here.
5. True – according to Dinah Rose, at least!

Workbook

7 Boxing idioms, page 16

4 Vocabulary check

You could ask a few personalised questions here as you're checking students' answers. For example: *Have any of you ever been in a boxing ring? How was it? Did you win? Are you ever sarcastic? Is your government doing anything that there's a lot of opposition to at the moment? Do you like taking risks?*

Answers

1. champion 2. ring 3. sarcastically
4. research 5. earn 6. opposition
7. taking 8. crime

Point out the Real English note: *If I were responsible ...*

5 Violent or dangerous?

Use the photos to ask if anyone has ever done climbing, snowboarding or canyoning.

Even though some of these activities are very obviously violent or dangerous, encourage students to explain why. For example, it could be argued that football is both violent and dangerous – players get into fights every now and then, they lose their tempers, they get their legs broken, and so on. Discussing these views helps extend students' vocabularies and develop their fluency.

Pairs or small groups can discuss each 'sport' while you move around the room to help with vocabulary when necessary. Perhaps make a note of language

that was lacking as students gave their views and present that language at the end of the discussion.

Workbook

4 Football and tennis, page 15

Photo opportunity

Idea 1. Ask groups to list what equipment is needed for each of the activities in the photos.

Idea 2. Divide the class into three groups – a rock climbing group, a footballing one and a snow-boarding one. Have each group list why they love their sport so much and then put the class into groups of three, asking them to try and persuade the people from the other groups why their chosen sport is the most exciting.

6 How-questions (G6)

This exercise introduces the important distinction between countable and uncountable nouns, which is one of the most important points in English grammar. It is discussed in detail in the Grammar Introduction on page 177 (see Grammar – the noun). If you have not already drawn students' attention to this section of the book, this is a good opportunity to do so.

You might want to point out to students that almost any adjective can be preceded by *How* in questions:

How cold is it outside?
> Not very. It's OK.

How unpleasant was having your tooth out, on a scale of 1 to 10?
> It was about 11!

Answers

1. long 2. far 3. long ago 4. much 5. long
6. well 7. hard/difficult/tough 8. often
9. many 10. serious/worried/nervous

Grammar check
1. many 2. much 3. many 4. many
5. much 6. much

7c 8a 9d 10b.

Between this lesson and the next, ask students to see how many other *How*-questions they can find or come up with.

Point out the Real English note: *Do you go clubbing much?*

Interviewing Jane Couch
If you want this section to last longer, put students in pairs and ask them to write 6 questions for Jane Couch. Then pool all these questions onto the board.

Students could then take turns with their partner pretending to be Jane Couch and ask half the questions each, before swapping roles. Encourage students to talk as much as possible and to try and use some of the vocabulary from this unit. If time is short, finish the class by pooling questions onto the board as above and then ask students to think about how they would answer them for homework. This will give them a chance to use dictionaries and to prepare their answers more. The next class could then begin with the role plays.

Workbook

10 Much and many 1, page 17
11 Much and many 2, page 17

7 Scottish Kickboxers

Before reading the text, ask students to list any martial arts they can think of and to describe how they differ from each other, where they come from originally, if anyone has ever studied any of them, etc. Help with vocabulary if necessary. Students could also discuss the benefits of learning a martial art, and which ones they personally prefer – if any!

You may want to read the text aloud while students follow in their books and then move straight to the Talking Point. Alternatively, you may want students to read the text silently with a simple task: *What happens when they fight against men?*

Remember, these texts are primarily for stimulating discussion. Don't let students get bogged down by new words.

Develop the theme in the Talking Point by asking: *Why aren't there any women motor racing drivers? Why do men tennis players earn almost double what the women earn? Is this fair?*

Photo opportunity

The colours of the kickboxers are the red, white and blue of the British team. In a multi-lingual class, ask what colours their national teams usually wear. In a mono-lingual class, ask if students know what colours these countries' sporting teams usually wear:

Ireland (green and white)
Germany (white and black)
Sweden (yellow and blue)
France (blue, white and red)
Brazil (gold, green and blue)
Holland (orange)
Poland (white and red)
Spain (dark red and blue)

8 Interests (G7)

This activity can be turned into a simple homework task. Students write about fifty words on a hobby they had as a child. This can be done in preparation for talking in small groups in the next lesson or as a follow-up to the class activity.

Workbook

5 Used to, page 15

9 Would and 'd (G8)

Encourage students to say these expressions several times chorally and individually until they can say them fluently:

I would if I could ...
I'd quite like to ...
If you'd rather ...
I wouldn't if I were you.
That'd be great.

Answers

1c 2e 3a 4b 5d

Grammar in context
1. I'd quite like to 2. That'd be great
3. I would if I could 4. If you'd rather
5. that'd be great 6. I would if I could
7. I'd quite like to 8. If you'd rather

Point out the Real English note.

10 Reaching decisions

These three role plays provide an opportunity to recycle language from Units 2a and 2b, as well as *would* expressions, such as: *So, what shall we do, then? We could always go ... I suppose we could ... Why don't we just ... To be honest with you, I'm not that keen on ... It's not really my thing.* Write this language on the board and encourage students to use it when doing the role plays.

Once students have discussed what they would do in each of the three situations, you could then ask them in pairs to write out one of the three conversations. This gives you a chance to monitor more closely and to help out with vocabulary, and it gives the students the chance to consolidate the new language.

Alternatively, students could begin by writing one of the conversations, as a way of preparing them for the stress of talking in real time.

Photo opportunity

See if any students know where this picture was taken (Brighton, on the south coast of England) and if any of them have ever been there. Students then discuss what kind of things they like seeing and doing when they go on holiday – how interested they are in going round old buildings, what they like to do in the daytime and at night, etc. If you have a multi-national class, students could also spend five minutes telling someone from a different country what their own home town has to offer tourists and visitors.

11 Checking you understand

When students are writing their own dialogues, make sure they write three-part exchanges, as in the exercise.

Answers

1. What? Do you mean just watching it or do you actually box yourself?
2. What? Do you mean just watching it or do you actually play yourself?
3. What? Do you mean just going to Chinese restaurants or do you actually make it yourself?
4. What? Do you mean just going to galleries or do you actually paint yourself?
5. What? Do you mean youth culture or Beethoven and things like that?

12 Boxing joke (T13)

Use the tape once or twice to show where the speaker pauses and uses intonation to tell the joke well. Encourage students to copy the way the speaker tells the joke. You might want to put students into groups of three or four and have them decide who tells it best.

Vocabulary Page

The vocabulary page can be used as either homework or classwork.

Idioms

1. cup 2. street 3. own 4. taste 5. accounting

a. It's not really my cup of tea.
b. It should be right up your street.
c. It's an acquired taste.
d. There's no accounting for taste. Oh well, each to their own.

Expressions with *thing*

1. one thing after another
2. don't know the first thing about
3. it's just one of those things
4. It's just not the done thing
5. the thing is
6. for one thing

Time expressions

1. morning 2. start 3. night 4. small
5. Last 6. dawn

All right

1c 2f 3b 4a 5d 6g 7e

Extra workbook exercises

3   Abbreviations, page 15
8   Books and newspapers, page 16
13   Paragraph ordering, page 18
15   Prepositions, page 19
16   *Go, play* or *do*, page 19
17   Writing, page 19

Review: Units 1 and 2

1 Tenses

1. I'm looking 2. likes 3. I do 4. She runs
5. I'm working 6. do you have

2 Multiple choice

1a 2a 3b 4a 5b 6b 7a 8b 9a 10b

3 Expressions

1. to tell you the truth 2. haven't you heard? 3. I
would if I could 4. I'm afraid I can't 5. one of those
things 6. not really keen

4 Conversation

1a 2c 3b 4h 5f 6g 7d 8e

5 Collocations

1e 2h 3g 4b 5a 6d 7f 8c

6 Adjectives

1e 2f 3h 4g 5c 6b 7i 8d 9a

7 Real English

1c 2a 3d 4g 5f 6h 7e 8b

8 Vocabulary quiz

1. A driving licence. 2. Ambitious. 3. Yes, but vegans
don't! 4.Very rarely. 5. Nowhere – they've stopped
working. 6. Untidy. 7. They commit suicide.
8. Yes, you do want to start a relationship.
9. A blonde. 10. In a pub or a bar. 11. Hardly ever.
12. About someone else's life. If you write a book
about your own life, it's your autobiography.
13. Commit them. 14. You get up very early in the
morning. 15. Their ideas are fixed in a negative way.
16. An only child. 17. No, they're just nice people to
live next door to. 18. You play one. 19. A ring.
20. Not very well.

Unit 3a
Big decisions

Unit overview

Topic

Asking and talking about decisions you have made.

The dialogue

Phil asks Jason about why he decided to become a
fireman and move to London.

Language input

- Question tags
- Questions with *why* and *How come – How
  come you left your job, then?*
- Explaining decisions – *I just got fed up with
  it.*
- Gerund and infinitive – *decided to leave,
  finished studying*
- Summarising – *So, you went to look for a
  job, then?*
- Saying you don't know – *I haven't got a clue.
  I've got no idea.*

Reading text

A woman from New Zealand explains why she came
to live in England.

The language strip

Here are some activities and questions for students to
exploit the language strip:

Divide the remarks into two groups: those which
start a new line in the conversation, and those which
are responses to what someone else has said.

Then try to add one line to some of the expressions
so they are two-line dialogues.

Are there any expressions where you understand all
the words in the expression, but you don't
understand the whole expression? If so, you may
want to learn the whole expression, and add it, with
an equivalent in your own language, to the
Expression Organiser on page 188.

1 Tough decisions

Before opening their books, ask students to think of
an important decision they have made (or have to
make), why they made it and how it turned out. Give
a few ideas if necessary: changing jobs, choosing a
university, buying a car etc. Perhaps tell them about a
big decision in your life and how it worked out. Give
the students a few minutes to think and make notes.

Ask if anyone would like to talk about their decision. Students should **not** be forced to talk about something they don't want to.

Tell the class that the unit they are going to look at will help them talk more fluently about decisions. Give students a few minutes to rank the decisions in the blue box on their own and then give them a few more minutes to explain their choices to a partner. You may want to help with relevant vocabulary such as *It must have been very difficult, It takes a long time to get over things like that.*

2 Who did what? (T14)

Before listening, ask the class to guess which of the decisions in the blue box they think the people in the pictures made. Listen to the tape, to see if their guesses were correct.

Answer

Speaker 1 decided to move house.
Speaker 2 decided to change her job.
Speaker 3 decided to stop smoking.

3 What a nightmare!

Listen again and ask them to write down the words or expressions which helped them work out which decisions were being talked about. Then ask the students if they can remember who said which of the six expressions listed. Before asking the class to use these expressions to talk about experiences they have had, check they remember how the phrases were used – what they were used to talk about. Refer to the tapescript on page 168 and ask students to find the expressions and underline them.

4 While you listen (T15)

Read the scene-setting introduction, but before playing the tape, draw students' attention to the heading 'Forty a day!' and ask them to guess what big decisions Phil and Jason might talk about. Without reading the dialogue, students then listen for the answers to questions 1 and 2. Let them discuss their answers in pairs. Then let them read the dialogue as you play the tape again. Then, in pairs, ask the students to fill in the first two or three gaps from memory before playing the tape with pauses so that they can check and fill in the missing words. Do this two or three gaps at a time until the end. Play the tape through one more time with students following the script. You may want students to read the dialogue, or parts of it, in pairs.

Answers

1. Jason decided to give up smoking, to become a fireman and to move to London.
2. He decided to give up smoking because it was destroying his lungs and he needed to pass the physical to get into the fire brigade. He joined the fire brigade because he wanted to do something exciting and different. He moved to London mostly because of work, but also because he was fed up with where he was living.

Workbook

4 I knew I'd have to . . . , page 21
5 Stuck, page 21
12 It's just as well . . . , page 24

Real English: Good for you!

You could quickly ask the students to think of some other situations when they could use this expression. (Somebody's managed to lose 3 kilos; passed an exam; decided to leave a job they hated, etc)

5 Talking Point

You can turn this into a more extensive discussion by splitting the class into three groups. One group lists reasons why some people decide to move to big cities; the second group lists reasons why some city dwellers decide to move to the countryside; the third group lists reasons why some people never even consider moving from where they grew up! Then put students in groups of three – one from each group – and ask them to share their ideas. Keep the class in these groups of three while they chat about the Talking Point questions.

6 Pronunciation (T16, side 2)

It is important to draw students' attention to the fact that even though these tags are called question tags, some are 'real' questions and some invite a comment to keep the conversation going. Students should notice that the last example is different in that it is a positive sentence with a positive tag. Tell them not to worry about this yet, as such tags are focused on in exercise 7.

7 Question tags (G9)

Answers

1. isn't it 2. is it 3. haven't we 4. didn't he 5. didn't it 6. did he 7. does it 8. didn't they

positive sentence = negative tag
negative sentence = positive tag

Positive-positive tags (G10)

Get students to read the mini-conversations in 1-4. The intonation of these tags could be up or down. It depends on how surprised the speaker is. The more surprised the speaker is, the more likely the intonation will be up. Beware of making black and white statements about intonation. It is better to talk about tendencies than rules.

Answers

1. did you 2. have you 3. are we 4. are you

An extension to this exercise is to ask students to write down three facts about themselves that no-one in the class knows or that they think might surprise other people in the class. They then walk around telling each other these facts and respond to each other using positive-positive tags. For example:

I was born in Kenya.
> You were born in Kenya, were you? I didn't know that.
Yes, my father used to work there.

Workbook

1 Question tags, page 20
2 You don't . . . , do you? page 20

8 Talking about jobs

Answers

The jobs in the pictures are: pilot, postman, police officer, surgeon, model, bouncer, fireman, mechanic, soldier

After identifying the jobs in the photos, model the next task for the class: *I wouldn't mind being a pilot. I imagine it would be really interesting. I could never be a soldier. I just couldn't kill anyone.* Point out the language used on page 42 and get students to talk about each photo and the other jobs in the blue box in pairs or small groups. After the group work, ask individuals to tell you which jobs they'd quite like to do or jobs they could never do and why.

A follow-up activity: use the photos to practise using *have to*. Write the following (or your own ideas) on the board:

You have to be fit.
You have to be quite intelligent.
You have to study for years and pass an exam.
You have to work long hours or shifts.
You have to have good people-skills.

Now discuss as a class or in small groups which statements apply to each job. This will also produce the negative *You don't have to be particularly fit.*

Workbook

6 What's the job? page 21

9 How come

This and the next exercise can both be done individually or in pairs, then checked in the whole class.

Answers

1. Why did you pay so much for your car?
2. Why did you get here so early?
3. Why did you refuse the invitation?
4. Why didn't you accept the job in LA?
5. Why are you so interested in Tibet?
6. Why isn't there any beer left in the fridge? /
   Why is there no beer left in the fridge?
7. how come 8. why 9. why 10. how come 11. why
12. how come

10 Explaining your decisions

Answers

a. We just got bored with each other.
b. I've always been interested in it.
c. I'd always wanted to.
d. I just got fed up with it.
e. I just felt like it.
f. A friend of mine recommended him.

1. I'd always wanted to,
2. A friend of mine recommended him
3. I just got fed up with it.
4. I just felt like it.
5. I've always been interested in it,
6. We just got bored with each other.

Once you have checked that the class have a-f correct, practise these expressions chorally and individually. It is important that students are able to say them easily and fluently as complete natural expressions. You might want the class to mark the main stresses in each sentence in their books.

To help students with the conversation activity at the bottom of page 44, you could tell them two or three things about yourself using some of these expressions, and recycling any other relevant language from this unit. You might also wish to draw students' attention to the Real English note before they discuss 1-5, and then encourage them to use *What on earth ...* questions if necessary when chatting.

Workbook

19 Collocations, page 26
Do this exercise together then use the sentences for more practice of *How come* questions and explaining decisions.

11 While reading

Before reading the text on page 45, tell the class they are going to read about someone who left New Zealand to come and live in England. Ask them to think of a few reasons why people might leave one country and go and live in another. Help with vocabulary where needed.

Answers

1. False – but she had been to England with her parents when she was six.
2. True.
3. False – she didn't really plan it.

12 Talking Point

For each of these questions, give students two or three minutes to think about their answers before they discuss them as a class or in small groups. A little preparation time can improve students' performance considerably. Encourage them to give reasons for their views.

13 Jokes! (T17)

1d   2a   3b   4c

14 Gerund and infinitive (G11)

This area is a potential minefield in classes and all teachers and students experience frustration at the seemingly arbitrary nature of gerunds and infinitives. When students read the examples using *remember*, ask them what the difference in meaning between the two sentences is. Try and elicit – or simply give – another couple of examples of things people typically say using each form. For example:

I can still remember feeling nervous before my first day at school.
I must remember to call my mum tomorrow.

It is useful for students to be given examples of these 'rules' in everyday use. You might want to ask the class to read G11 before trying the task, as it clarifies some of the more confusing words, such as *remember* and *try*, and also gives typical examples. You will also need to point out that *love* and *prefer* are followed by gerunds to talk about general tastes:

I really love being able to have a lie-in on Sundays.
My husband likes being around the house but I prefer getting out in the fresh air.

However, to talk about tastes and preferences on specific occasions, we usually add *would* to the verb, and then use an infinitive to follow:

I'd love to go to Greece again this summer.
We could go out tonight, if you want, but personally, I'd just prefer to stay in.

Begin and *start* can be followed by either gerund or infinitive without any change in meaning, although *begin* is more generally followed by an infinitive, and *start* is more generally followed by a gerund.

When running through the answers, you may want to add a typical example for each. For example:

I'll ask him to do it when I see him.

Students will learn the 'rules' best through such everyday natural examples.

Verb check

Answers

1. G/I   2. I   3. I   4. G   5. G/I   6. I   7. G/I
8. G/I   9. G   10. G   11. G/I   12. G/I   13. G
14. I   15. G/I   16. I

Grammar check

Answers

1. to learn   2. to go   3. in travelling   4. with working
5. with doing   6. to get   7. to go

Grammar in context

This exercise revises the forms presented in the Grammar Check within the context of talking about decisions. One fun way to start this exercise is to put students in pairs and ask them first to think of the most predictable answers that people might give to question 1. For example:

I wanted to do something different. I was fed up with doing the same thing, day in, day out.

Write these answers on the board, helping with vocabulary where necessary. Then ask them to think of the funniest or strangest answers they can to the question – *I wanted to become a crocodile trainer. I decided to retire at 22*, etc. They can then answer the other questions as they wish.

Possible answers

1. I wanted to do something different for a change.
   I was fed up with doing the same old thing, day in, day out.

2. I was bored with Bournemouth!
   I was interested in the fashion industry, and thought it would be a good place to study it.
3. I wanted a bit more freedom than he/she was giving me.
   I didn't want to settle down just yet.
4. I was interested in ballet and jazz step and things and wanted to take that further.
   I hoped I might one day get to be in 'Cats', my favourite musical!

The watersports in the photos are: snorkelling, surfing, windsurfing, jetskiing

Workbook

7 Infinitive or *-ing* form, page 22
8 Quick verb check, page 22

15 Summarising

This exercise gets students to practise turning a deduction the listener feels fairly sure about, into a summarising question. You might want to begin by asking students to look at the example in the blue box and then asking them to find an example of this in the conversation between Phil and Jason. (Phil asks *Oh, right. So he helped you, did he?*)

Answers

1. So you think you got the job, then?
2. So you wanted to play in a band, then?
3. Right, so you thought it would help your career, then?
4. So you think you failed, then?
5. So you're not going into work, then?

Talking Point

Tell the class that everybody tells little white lies from time to time and that they're useful if you don't want to hurt people's feelings. Maybe begin the discussion by giving a couple of examples from your own life!

Workbook

3 I shouldn't have done that, page 20
This amusing story relates to the Talking Point and practises the structure *should've done / shouldn't have done*.

16 Playing for time (T18)

When practising the pronunciation, make sure students sound hesitant! For questions 1-5, students are **not** expected to have real answers, although

obviously some may. The important point is to practise using the expressions confidently.

17 Role Play

This gives students a chance to recycle a lot of the language presented in this unit in a fun context. Put the class in pairs and give them time to prepare the questions they would like to ask the famous person they have elected to interview, **before** selecting someone to pretend to be this famous person. This keeps the whole class as involved in the task as possible.

A homework task that follows on from this is to write an imaginary interview with a different celebrity – each student choosing someone they like and know about – trying to use as much of the language from this unit as possible.

18 Saying you don't know (T19)

Practise the examples highlighted in red and the expressions that students underline to help students answer the general knowledge questions more fluently.

Answers

1b 2a 3f 4h 5c 6g 7e 8d

An extension of the final task is to ask each student to write three general knowledge questions about their country (for multi-national classes) or about something they are particularly interested in and then to ask a few different partners these questions. This not only gives students the chance to re-use the phrases from exercises 16 and 18, but also empowers them by bringing in their own knowledge and areas of expertise to the class!

General knowledge

Answers

1. France, Canada (Quebec), Ivory Coast, Algeria, Cameroon, Mozambique, (parts of) Belgium
2. 62.1 miles
3. 1240 million (approx!)
4. Ukraine, Russia, Moldova, Kazakhstan, Uzbekistan, Georgia, Belorussia, Turkmenistan
5. drake, bitch, kid, sow
6. Northern Greece

19 Talking Point

Start the discussion in pairs. Give three or four minutes for everyone to give their opinion, then ask each pair to join another pair to make groups of (about) four and see if they agree on how much correction should take place. Then have a whole class discussion.

Whilst the choice presented to the students here is stark, it should raise some interesting points. Some students may feel that continuous correction is desirable – a feeling often remedied by actually stopping them every time they make any kind of mistake and instantly correcting it! It is also useful for you as a teacher to explain your own attitudes to correction at this point. The main goal for students when talking should be mutual intelligibility, and any correction in class should take this into account. Over-correction can be discouraging and lead to a loss of motivation. Also, students talking freely provides a great opportunity for teachers to listen for phrases, collocations and words that students have still only half-learned, as well as typical grammar mistakes. Make a note of these problems and bring them to students' attention later. These can be written on the board and students encouraged to correct the mistakes themselves. It is probably better to interrupt students to correct them only if there are obvious signs of communication breakdown.

For further ideas on the whole topic of correction, see *Correction* by Mark Bartram and Richard Walton, published by LTP, ISBN 0 906717 91 4.

Workbook
13 Writing, page 24
Ask students to do this for homework.

Unit 3b
Flying

Unit overview

Topic

Flying!

The text

A woman tries to have a secret smoke on a plane.

Language input

- Vocabulary connected with flying
- Past perfect continuous for giving explanations – *I'd been thinking about it for a while.*
- Strong comparatives – *It was much better than I thought it would be.*
- Strong adjectives – *Scary – it was terrifying!*
- Second conditionals

Vocabulary page

The language strip

Ask students to find language used by airline staff and crew when you go on a flight. Then ask them to find things a passenger might say.
Which of the expressions would you see, not hear?

Lead in

To lead in to the theme of the unit, ask students to look at the pictures and then discuss the following questions:

Have you ever flown? Who with? Why did you choose that airline? What do you think the best airline is? Why? Do you like airports? Why / why not?

Then start the first activity.

1 Your captain speaking

When checking the true or false statements, you may want to ask, *Are you sure?* and encourage the use of these responses:

Yes, definitely.
I'm pretty / fairly sure.
No, I'm not too sure.

Give the students a few more minutes to discuss 1-8 in pairs and then discuss these points together, concentrating on the structures:

You're not allowed to smoke during take-off and landing.
Smoking is not allowed / is strictly forbidden during take-off and landing.

Answers

1. False, but you must say at check-in who packed your luggage if you didn't do it yourself.
2. False 3. True 4. False 5. True 6. True

Other rules

1. Smoking is not allowed during take-off and landing. In fact, most flights are completely non-smoking these days.
2. You may use a CD player. (Some airlines do not allow this.)
3. You have to take off high-heeled shoes in an emergency because they damage the escape chute.
4. Hand luggage must either be kept in the overhead lockers or under the seat in front of you.
5. You can use the toilet at any time except when the seatbelt sign is on, when you have to remain in your seat.
6. Seats must be in the upright position during take-off and landing.
7. You only need to have your seatbelt on when the seatbelt sign is on.
8. There are special seatbelts for babies which must be used when the seatbelt sign is on.

2 Vocabulary

These words all come from the text on page 50. As the students are discussing what they think the article is going to be about, monitor and help students put some of the vocabulary into whole sentences. Write some of the predictions on the board. Tell the class they're going to read an article about a woman whose desperate need (perhaps teach the word *craving*) for a smoke landed her in big trouble – at 30,000 feet. Next let them read the text to see how it compares with their predictions. In pairs, let them answer questions 1-3 from Exercise 3. Encourage the class to answer in their own words.

Answers

air travel: touched down, nervous, refuelling, cabin crew, on board
the law: handcuffed, prosecuted, fined, arrested
smoking: light up, puff

3 While reading

Answers

1. Because she was so nervous she felt she just had to have a smoke to calm her down.
2. When the plane finally landed at Heathrow.
3. She was handcuffed. She was prosecuted and then fined £440.

Photo opportunity

Page 50: Once the class have finished Exercise 3 and read the text, ask them to look at the photo and discuss who the smoker is: male or female – how do they know? (long fingernails, the shape of her lips) and what sort of age? This could lead into a discussion on various related topics:

- What age do people start smoking?
- Why do people start smoking?
- How are cigarettes advertised? (You could bring in advertisements from magazines to discuss.)

The class might also like to discuss which of them smoke, why, when they started, if they've ever tried to stop, how, and so on.

4 Word check

Give the paragraph references if you want this activity to take less time.

Answers

1. handled (paragraph 2)
2. sign (paragraph 3)
3. relations (paragraph 4)
4. expecting (paragraph 5)
5. fuss (paragraph 5)

5 Comprehension check

Answers

1. Because she's a nervous passenger. She said she couldn't have handled the flight without a cigarette.
2. No, she wouldn't have taken the flight if she'd known about the non-smoking rule beforehand.
3. No, but she turned violent once the plane had landed at Heathrow, where the police were called.
4. No, because she said that the fine was much higher than she'd expected and that it was a lot of fuss to make over a couple of cigarettes!

6 Collocations

This could be set for homework if you want to move on from the text. Setting this as a homework task has the advantage of making students re-visit the text later on.

Answers

1. twice 2. taken 3. attracted 4. touched 5. turned
6. touched 7. turned 8. attracted 9. taken 10. twice

7 Talking Point

Choose some, not all, of these discussion points. Perhaps write the ones you want the class to discuss on the board and give students a few minutes to think about their responses and even make a few notes before discussing in small groups or as a class.

Alternatively, put the class into small groups and let the groups decide which three questions they would like to talk about.

8 Flying vocabulary

Answers

1g 2f 3b 4c 5j 6a 7h 8i 9d 10e

Workbook

20 Airports and planes, page 26

Extension activity

After the class have finished Exercise 8 and chatted about the questions at the foot of page 51, discuss what they think the photo here shows, where this billboard might be and why a company like Telefonica might choose to advertise on the way out of an airport. Then tell them to imagine they have been on a flight where there were problems with some of the things mentioned in exercise 8. Give them 5 minutes to decide what these problems were and to make a few notes. Then put the students in pairs, and ask them to role play a phone conversation between someone who has just got off that flight and their husband/wife. For homework, students could then write up the conversation they had, and could even role play it again at the start of the following lesson with a different partner. Remember that repeating the same task once or twice usually improves students' performance.

9 Giving explanations (G12)

Grammar in context

This exercise practises the past perfect continuous within the context of talking about decisions. 1-6 is basically straight manipulation of form, but you might want to exploit other details:

• You could briefly check that the class remember how to restructure the questions in 3 and 4 as *why*-questions.

• You could also ask a few vocabulary-related questions, like:

In number 4, why does the first speaker add, 'if you don't mind me asking'? Can you think of any other questions you could add this phrase to?

What's the fixed expression used at the end of number 2? (give it a go)
What other kinds of things might you 'splash out on' apart from a computer?

Answers

1. I'd been reading
2. I'd been thinking, they'd been trying
3. I'd been doing
4. we'd been arguing
5. I'd been living
6. we'd been having

The time expressions are:

1. since Sally told me about her trip
2. for a while/for ages
3. for years
4. for months
5. since I left home
6. for a while

Grammar pairwork

When students are coming up with answers to these questions, encourage them to follow the extended turns they saw in 1-6. For example, a possible answer for a. might be: *Well, her mum had been asking us about it for ages, and I'd been thinking about it too so we just decided to go ahead.* Point out that the past perfect continuous is often followed by a past simple clause introduced by *so*.

Before students talk about a big decision in their life, you could model the task for them by talking about a big decision you have made, and use this opportunity to recycle language from Unit 3a. Then encourage the class to tell a few different people about a decision they have made. This is a repeat of the task at the beginning of 3a but students have had more input since then and so you have the chance to see if their performance is improving. Remember that telling and retelling helps students develop fluency and get used to using new vocabulary and grammar.

Point out the Real English note: *Basically, ...*

Photo opportunity

Page 52: After students have discussed the question under the Real English note, ask:

Have you ever bought a second-hand car? When? How much for? Did it work OK? Would you ever buy one? Have you ever bought anything else second-hand? How do you feel about haggling over prices?

Find out if anyone has a recent example of haggling over the price of something.

10 Adjectives

Strong comparatives

This exercise practises one way in which comparatives are often used in everyday speech. Before students try 1-6, you could practise the mini-conversations presented above, paying particular attention to the way the phrases in red are stressed. While there are no definite answers for 1-6, some answers are more probable than others. Here are some likely answers, but allow others too if they make sense.

Possible answers

1. Oh, it went well – much better than I'd expected.
2. Yeah, it was sweltering – much hotter than I thought it would be.
3. Great – much easier than I'd expected.
4. Oh, it went well – much better than I'd expected.
5. It was fine – much nicer than I thought it would be.
6. Yeah, it was really interesting – much better than I'd expected.

Workbook

14 Comparatives, page 24

Strong adjectives (T20)

You might like to ask students if they can think of any other weak/strong pairs that they could use like this, for example:

not very nice / disgusting, difficult / impossible, silly / ridiculous

You could ask the class to write mini-conversations like those in 1-8 using any extra pairs of adjectives that they think of.

Get students to read the tapescript of the conversations (page 169) as you play the tape. Then get them to read the conversations in pairs.

Answers

1. Hot? It was boiling!
2. Big? It's enormous!
3. Cold? It's freezing!
4. Quiet? It's dead!
5. Surprised? I was shocked!
6. Small? It's tiny!
7. Good-looking? He's gorgeous!
8. Scary? It was terrifying!

Follow-up comments:

a8 b3 c2 d6 e1 f4 g7 h5

11 Second conditionals (G13)

After the class have added the six verbs to the blue box, encourage a discussion on the point made here. *Is it really true that we all use second conditionals too much? Is wishful thinking a waste of time?* What kind of second conditionals do students often find themselves saying to themselves? Why?

Answers

The missing words are:

earned, had, met, wasn't/weren't, wanted, didn't exist

1. I'm sure Rachel would understand if you explained it to her.
2. If we had more time, we could look round the museums.
3. The fact is I'd buy one if it wasn't / weren't so expensive.
4. I often think that if I didn't have any children, I'd travel round the world.
5. I often think that life would be easier if everybody just told the truth.

Likely or unlikely

This brief exercise is to encourage students to be aware of the fact that grammar is a matter of choice, and depends on how the speaker sees the events they are describing. See G13 for more examples of the strange choices people make when deciding which conditionals to use!

Answers

1. If I met 2. If everybody thought 3. If I live
4. If I lived

a4 b1 c2 d3

Workbook

9 Second conditionals, page 23
10 *Wish* and conditionals, page 23
11 Famous conditionals, page 23

12 Flying joke (T21)

Let students read the joke through and try to decide on possible endings before you play the cassette. Pause the tape before the blanked-out punchline and ask the class to shout out their endings. Then give the class the punchline, before getting them to practise telling the whole joke to each other in pairs. The punchline is at the top of page 192.

The worst flying story doesn't necessarily have to be something that has actually happened to students. It could be a news item, an urban myth or even other flying jokes. Bring in a few of your own just in case ideas are in short supply. The internet is always a great source of such items.

Remind students to use section 3b of the Expression Organiser on page 188.

Vocabulary page

Decisions, decisions

1. right 2. immediate 3. wise 4. wrong
5. unpopular 6. joint

Smoking

a. smoker b. cigarette c. cigarettes d. cigarette
e. smoking

1. heavy, occasional 2. give up, started 3. put out
4. ends 5. advertising 6. smoking

Watch, see, look

1. see 2. see, looks 3. watch 4. seen 5. watch 6. look
7. watch 8. see 9. seen 10. looked, see

Idioms

1. cake 2. stone 3. nothing 4. depth 5. sailing
6. done

Extra workbook exercises

15 Expressions with *in*, page 25
16 Encouraging expressions, page 25
17 Phrasal verbs with *up*, page 25
18 Expressions with *mind*, page 26

Unit 4a
Your weekend

Unit overview

Topic

Talking about plans and intentions for the weekend.

The dialogue

Steve and Ken discuss their plans for the coming weekend.

Language input

- Collocations with *go* – *I'm going away, I'm going out, I'm going on a ... ,* etc
- The future – *'ll, going to,* present continuous, present simple, etc
- Spoken grammar – *I've got somebody coming round, I've got to do some shopping* etc
- Vocabulary – *meeting, appointment, date*

Reading text

Surfing the net – skydiving and taking risks

Learning advice

Throughout *Innovations* there are many reminders of the importance of noticing and recording multi-word items, such as collocations and other expressions. Page 56 provides an opportunity to re-emphasise this and to remind learners of the importance of using the Expression Organiser on pages 187 – 191.

The language strip

Use some of these questions to exploit the strip.

Which expressions are in the present continuous? Why? Which do you think you are most likely to say on a Friday?
Find three things that you often do at the weekend.
Find all the questions and write a response to each one.

Lead in

Use the photos on page 57 to lead in to the unit. Ask the class about each picture:

- *What is the place shown in picture 1?* (a theatre box office) *How often do you go to the theatre?*
- *What is happening in picture 2? What's in the buggy? Where's the baby? Do you have to spend ages waiting outside clothes shops for your partner?*
- In picture 3, perhaps ask about the girls' faces – they look very serious. *What's going on?*

Ask students if they ever spend their weekends doing things like this. This leads in very nicely to exercise 1.

1 A typical weekend

Students can do this alone, then compare with a partner. Help with time adverbs such as *most weekends, almost every weekend*, etc. Encourage students to say a bit more about each thing that they actually do – how often they do it? Where?

Point out the Real English note: *What are you up to this weekend?* You may want to ask a few students: *What are you up to this evening?* Or let them ask you.

2 Planning expressions (T22)

Students will probably need to hear the tape two or three times. Once they have ticked the expressions they heard Gavin use, you could ask students in pairs to reconstruct as much as they can remember about Gavin's plans for the weekend, using the expressions ticked. Then read T22 on page 169 together and ask them to underline the expressions. The pairs then use any of the expressions on page 57 to chat about their own plans for the coming weekend.

Answers

The expressions Gavin uses are, in order:
I guess I'll probably
I'm going to try to
Unfortunately, I've got to
I imagine I'll
I guess I'll probably

3 Before you listen (T23)

Read the introduction to set the scene. Students listen to the tape once without reading the dialogue and then discuss the question in pairs. Next, let them read the dialogue as you play the tape again. Then, in pairs, ask the students to fill in the first two or three gaps from memory before you play the tape again, this time with pauses so that they can check and fill in the missing words. Do this two or three gaps at a time until the end. Play the tape through one more time with students following the script. Remember that listening to the same language again and again is vital for students who want to improve their spoken English. You may want students to read the dialogue, or parts of it, in pairs.

Answers

Steve is going out for dinner with his parents tonight to a little French place near his house. He's got to get up early on Saturday to do some cooking and to clean the house, because he's got some people coming over. They'll probably go and see a film in the evening. Ken is probably just going to stay in tonight, because on Saturday night he's going to a party on a boat. On Sunday, he's got to do some things for work.

When the class are asking about any phrases in the conversation that they have not met before, use this opportunity to extend and develop their lexicons where possible. for example, if a student asks what *dragging on* means, write on the board *This week's been dragging on forever*, explain that this means that it has been a long, slow, difficult week. Then ask if they can think of anything else that can drag on forever – meetings, lessons, films, lectures, etc, and write a couple of these examples on the board as well. Encourage students to record this kind of expression with two or three examples in their vocabulary notebooks.

Workbook

1 Future arrangements, page 27
You might want to give this for homework.

4 Talking Point

Take up one or more of the Talking Points. Then use the pictures along the bottom of pages 58 and 59. Ask students if any of the activities pictured here are part of anyone's weekends.

> *Do any of you ever do parachute jumps (or anything similar)? Walk along the beach? Go sailing? Go flying? Go for a drive? Wash your car? Go to the market and do the shopping? Work out in the gym? When? How often?*

This is a good chance for students to re-use some of the time expressions from page 29. If anyone in the class does something particularly interesting or strange at the weekend, you could recycle the *How-*questions from page 33, by having the rest of the class ask such questions to interview the student. The interviewee may want to use some of the delayers on page 47 when answering.

5 Vocabulary check

The problem for students with groups of words like this is they all seem to have very similar meanings – they all involve meeting people! The difference lies in the collocations, the way these words work with other words. As you check the answers with the class, try and elicit other possible endings for each of 1-8. For example, in number 1 we might also say *with Dr. Jones for five o'clock* or *with the optician tomorrow*, but we certainly wouldn't say *with a friend of mine later*. Encourage students to write down whole expressions with these words in their notebooks.

Explain that remembering natural examples is just as important as remembering what words mean.

Answers

The main difference is to do with usage and collocation. You *have a meeting* with your boss or with clients – it's usually work-related. You'd usually *make / have an appointment* with a dentist, doctor or optician, although if you're going to an office to see a particular person, you might *have an appointment*. You *go on / have a date* with someone you're attracted to.

1. an appointment
2. a meeting or an appointment (you make an appointment to have a meeting!)
3. a meeting
4. a date
5. an appointment

1c 2d 3a 4b 5f 6e 7h 8g

Workbook

6 Collocations, page 28

Point out the Real English note: *a friend's*. Ask students how they would say this in their own language.

6 Talking Point

This gives students a chance to personalise the vocabulary presented in 5. You may wish to provide a couple of examples that are true for you, just to model the kind of language students can use. Then let them discuss the questions in small groups.

7 Collocations with *go*

Go is one of the most commonly used verbs in English, and this exercise aims to extend students' ability to use it in its many different patterns. There are two personalisation sections: firstly, students use six of the collocations to tell their partner something about their plans for the weekend. Secondly, they discuss the questions that follow. Encourage students to continue these conversations as much as possible. Then ask them to transfer the correct collocations into their notebooks.

Answers

The wrong collocations are:
1. shopping tonight
2. my friend's up in Yorkshire
3. shopping
4. the pub
5. driving
6. some shopping

8 Pronunciation (T24)

Emphasise the importance of saying *'ll*, not *will*. *I'll see you later* is the normal, natural way of saying it, whereas *I will see you later* means something different, with its suggestion of contradiction or emphasis.

Play all the sentences through once, with students reading silently as they listen. Play the tape a second time and stop after each example for choral and individual repetition.

9 The future (G14)

There is still a common misconception that *will* is the future form in English and this exercise sets out to redress this. When trying to decide which future form to use, it is vital to bear in mind **why** the speaker thinks the event being described is going to happen – is something scheduled, like a timetable, is it an arrangement already made, and so on. The best time to refer the class to G14 on page 181 is after the Grammar discussion. G14 provides a few more natural examples which serve as valuable additional input.

Answers

Four different future forms
a. going to
b. present simple
c. present continuous
d. 'll

Grammar discussion
1. earlier, before now
2. it's a timetabled fact
3. now, at the moment of speaking!
4. yes, they know about it already

Grammar check

Once students have tried 1-6 on their own, ask them to discuss in pairs how they reached their decisions. When going through the answers, draw attention to the context in each that helps you decide which form to choose. For example, in number 4 the present continuous would probably be used as the speaker is discussing arrangements (s)he has already made.

The answers given are probable, but remember that the forms the speaker chooses depend on how the speaker perceives the event at the time of speaking. The same event can be perceived in more than one way.

Answers

1. I'll do 2. gets in 3. I'll do 4. I'm going
5. is going to give 6. I'm going to sneeze

Grammar in context

This exercise uses the structures to talk about plans for the weekend – the topic of this unit. Encourage students to try to learn **whole sentences** from these examples, particularly those which they can imagine needing to use in the future.

Remembering whole examples probably helps students acquire a better intergrammar in the long term.

Answers

1c 2a 3d 4b 5h 6g 7e 8f

Workbook

There are plenty of exercises based on the Future:
1 Future arrangements, page 27
2 Will / won't, page 27
3 'll and *be going to*, page 27
4 Try and . . . , page 28
5 Asking about plans, page 28
7 Reading – future forms, page 29
8 Time prepositions, page 29
16 Going to have to . . . , page 32
Give these for homework one or two at a time as you work through the unit.

Surfing the net

Remember that these texts are primarily to stimulate reaction and discussion rather than for detailed comprehension and vocabulary work.

Before reading this article, ask the class how many ways we use the word *surf (surf the net, surfing, wind-surfing)*. Then ask the class to look at the picture and discuss what's going on. What would you call this activity – sky-surfing? (Make sure everyone notices the laptop on the surfboard.)

Ask them what they would like to know about the two men in the picture. Put some of the student-generated questions on the board. Then ask the class to read the first paragraph only and see how many of their questions were answered.

Then write the three paragraph headings on the board:

> *The question everyone asks*
> *How fast do you fall?*
> *Why do people do it?*

Predict together what the answers are before students read the rest of the text. Checking these answers leads directly into the Talking Point.

10 Talking Point

Give students time to think about their answers before discussing in small groups or as a class.

11 Spoken grammar (G15) (T25)

After reading the four examples in the blue box, look at G15 on page 181, before students try 1-8 in pairs.

Probable answers

1. I've got a friend coming round to help me with my homework on Sunday.
2. I'm supposed to be going shopping with a friend on Saturday, but I'll probably give it a miss.
3. I might be going to the cinema, but I'm not really sure yet.
4. I've got to get this essay written this weekend.
5. I've got to clean my flat up a bit this weekend.
6. Steve might be having a party tomorrow night.
7. I'm supposed to be meeting some friends on Sunday for lunch, but I don't really know if I'll feel up to it.
8. I've got my mother coming round on Saturday afternoon.

12 Role play

The photograph is taken at a horse-racing event.

For this role play to really work, you will need to spend a few minutes exploring common ways of inviting people, as exemplified in the blue box. Usually, the speaker mentions the event – *We're going to have a party next weekend* – and then extends an invitation – *and we'd love you to come along, if you're free.* Draw students' attention to the five-step conversation that occurs:

1. invitation
2. polite refusal + reason
3. asking if these plans could be changed
4. saying they can't
5. closing comment

In pairs, get students to write a short dialogue following this pattern using the phrases highlighted in red. Then get the class walking around inviting each other to a variety of different events using 5-step conversations.

Photo opportunity

This photo could help start a discussion on various topics:

> *1. Do you think horse-racing is cruel?*
> *2. Have you ever bet on a horse?*
> *3. How do you feel about gambling? Do you or would you do these things: bet on a football match? buy a lottery ticket? spend an evening in a casino? buy and sell shares on the stock market? buy a house hoping that the value will rise? Are these all gambling?*

In what way are they different? Do you disapprove of any of them?

4. What is the largest amount of cash you have ever had in your hands? Why did you have it?

The text and Talking Point on page 61 is a related topic – taking risks. You could follow up all this discussion with a written homework task. Students have to write 50-100 words on either of the following: *People like taking risks because ...* or *People place bets and gamble because ...* Give the students some key verb + noun collocations to help them with ideas:

> *take risks, break the monotony, make a change, give you something to look forward to, make a lot of money, escape from everyday life, get a kick out of it*

13 Plan a weekend

This is a fun chance for students to put some of the grammar and vocabulary they have learned in this unit into practice. Before students plan a weekend on their own, get them to read about Gavin's weekend (T22, page 169) again to remind them of the kind of language they will need when telling others about their plans.

When planning a cheap weekend with a partner, the language needed to make decisions will involve phrases like *Why don't we ... ?, Would you like to ... ?, Shall we ... ? , I'd really like to ...*, while reporting decisions to another partner will more likely require the present continuous and *going to*. This fluency work, therefore, provides an opportunity to assess how well students are using these structures and you could round up the activity by focusing on some typical errors in a general class feedback session.

Festivals

You could use these photos to start discussions on these topics:

> 1. *Do people do anything for Hallowe'en in your country? Is it harmless fun or is there an unpleasant side to it?*
> 2. *Do the pictures match your ideas of what traditional Scottish culture is? What else do you know about Scotland and the Scots?*
> 3. *What are the most interesting festivals in your own country, region or town?*
> 4. *Is traditional culture still important to people in your country or region? What does it mean to you personally? Is it used to sell your country as a tourist destination? Give some examples.*

These photos also provide an opportunity to practise the structure *They look* + adjective. Ask students to write down three possible endings to this sentence to describe the people pictured and to then compare their answers. *They look brilliant / a bit scary / very serious / quite young.*

14 Famous futures

Many students will listen to plenty of pop music with English lyrics, some of which will provide great examples of future forms. After completing 1-4, you could ask the class to go home and try to find some more songs with future forms in them for homework, to make a note of them and to think about why particular verb forms are used. Start the next class by asking students to share their findings.

Note that many British speakers of English also use *gonna* in informal conversation, even though some people still frown on it!

With the right class, some of these quotes could be used to lead into further discussions. The George Bernard Shaw quote might lead to a debate about who should rule the world – More young people? More women? More people from different kinds of backgrounds? What difference would it make? Which leaders are most in touch? Most out of touch?

Similarly, the Voltaire quote could be used to lead into a discussion on the pros and cons of censorship. Is there a limit to how much freedom of speech people should have? Should neo-Nazis be allowed a platform to spread their views? Should TV give extremist organisations a voice? Why/why not?

If you wish to set up debates like this, brainstorm ideas and write useful collocations on the board before the discussion itself begins. You can also then consolidate any discussion by setting a related written homework.

Unit 4b
Party animals

Unit overview

Topic

Parties

The text

A rave party goes through the floor into the flat below.

Language input

- Using *just – I just couldn't wait. We're just going to have lunch.*
- Planning expressions – *I'll bring some music if you sort out the food.*

Role play

Planning a party

Vocabulary page

The language strip

Ask students to divide the expressions into two groups: those most likely to be said by the person giving the party and those most likely to be said by a guest. (Some could fit either category.)

Lead in

If you asked students to look for song lyrics with future verb forms (page 63) for homework, begin by getting them to report back.

1 What kind of party?

To lead into Unit 4b ask students: *What was the last party you went to? What kind of party was it?* Spend a few minutes letting students tell everyone about their last party then put them in pairs to discuss the questions in exercise 1. Help with vocabulary when needed and point out the Real English notes. Encourage them to talk as much as possible about what each type of party involves for them personally. For example, *What happens when you have a big family get-together? Where would it usually be? Who comes? Is there food? Drink? How often do you have them?* You may also need to make sure that the class know the verbs to talk about these parties: I *went to* a friend of mine's stag night. I *went to* a friend of mine's birthday party. We *have* dinner parties quite regularly.

After students have read the Real English notes, ask the class to look at the photos on pages 65 and 66. Ask: *Do you have clubs like this in your country? Do you*

ever go to them? Why | Why not? What kind of music do you think is being played? Do you like that kind of thing? Why | why not?

Photo opportunity

Body piercing seems to be increasing in popularity in many countries. As a fun task, put students in pairs and ask them to find some pierced body parts in the photo on page 65. If you look closely, you will see that the man on the left has his right nipple and left ear pierced, as does the man in the middle.

2 Collocations

With a higher level class, extend their use of these collocations. For example, after number 3, ask what else apart from a demonstration can *get out of hand*, and what the consequences of that might be. Similarly, after number 5, you could ask the class if they can think of any incidents in their country recently that have *led to calls for tighter laws* on a particular issue.

Answers

1. ended in tragedy
2. lose control
3. got out of hand
4. organised crime
5. led to calls for tighter laws
6. suffering from shock

3 While reading

Before students answer 1-3 in pairs, give them a few sentence starters on the board for giving personal responses to the text. For example:

I can't believe that ...
I think that the worst | funniest | most frightening thing about this article is the fact that ...

Then give the class time to discuss their own reaction to what they read.

Answers

1. The roof of his flat collapsed, and over a hundred people fell through from the flat upstairs into his living room.
2. The biggest fear is that raves are the kind of places where people take drugs, and if there's a demand for drugs, then organised crime will inevitably get involved. It's this connection that worries police the most.
3. No, not at all. In fact, many of them actually just carried on dancing, as if nothing had happened.

4 Comprehension check

Ask students to try to answer 1-6 on their own without looking back at the text and then compare their answers with a partner. If there are differences, let them look back at the text to clear these problems up. When running through the answers, repeat the vocabulary in the text that helped students make their decisions – *the party was held in a deserted flat; the techno music being played weakened the structure of the floor*, etc to reinforce useful collocations.

Answers

1. No, Tribal Spiral held the party in an unoccupied flat they'd taken over just for the party.
2. No, it was the loud techno music that weakened the structure.
3. No, he lived in the flat downstairs.
4. No, he's still waiting for someone from the council to come round and fix it.
5. No, there's been a whole flood of complaints.
6. No, lots of people carried on dancing – even when the ambulancemen arrived.

Workbook

9 It's a great place . . . , page 30
10 Myself, page 30
13 Weak – weaken, page 31

5 Talking Point

Some of these questions could easily be developed into debates or written homework. The issue of what could or should be done about drug-taking works well as a class debate with certain groups, and gives you a chance to introduce useful collocations such as:

a rise in recreational drug use, differentiate between hard and soft drug use, call for tougher sentences, put more money into drug awareness campaigns, it's a complex issue.

The issue of organised crime could also be treated in a similar way.

Alternatively, after the Talking Point, you could develop the theme of music. Give the class a list of common sentences for talking about why you like or don't really like different types of music:

It's a bit too repetitive for me.
It's not really my cup of tea.
It's got no tune.
It's great to dance to.
It's got a good beat.
It's very relaxing.
I love his/her voice etc.

Ask students in pairs or threes to discuss what they think about different kinds of music.

Before you play any recorded music in class, check that this is not illegal.

6 Just (G16) (T26)

After you have practised sentences 1–6, you might like to refer the class to G16 on page 182, then ask them to decide in which sentences *just* has been used to make the statement sound unimportant or uninteresting (1, 2, 3 and 5) and in which it is used to mean *at this very moment* (4 and 6).

Similarly, once the class have added *just* to 1-8, you could practise the sentences and then ask the class to make the same kind of decisions. In examples 1, 3, 5, 6 and 8, *just* is used to make the statements sound unimportant or uninteresting; in 2, 4 and 7 *just* is used to mean *at this or that very moment*.

Answers

The word *just* suggests the action or thing that follows is unimportant or normal or unexciting. In number 6, the speaker is using a mobile phone.

1. There's nothing to worry about. It's just a dog barking.
2. I won't be a minute. I'm just going to the loo.
3. Who's that at the door? Oh, it's just William!
4. I tried to ring you on my mobile phone just after the plane landed.
5. There's nothing seriously wrong with you, Mr. Brown. It's just old age – nothing else!
6. I'll just be a minute or two.
7. We're just going to have lunch.
8. I don't feel like much to eat – just a sandwich and a cup of coffee.

7 I just couldn't wait

Answers

1. I just couldn't wait.
2. I just couldn't believe my eyes.
3. I just couldn't make up my mind.
4. I just couldn't bear it any longer.
5. I just couldn't resist them.

After exercise 7, but before exercise 8, ask the class if this boot is the kind of thing they *just couldn't resist*? Then put the men in the class into one group, the women in another. Tell them they've all been on a shopping spree and are feeling guilty. They are going to come home to their partner and explain that they *just couldn't resist* buying a few things. Ask each group to make a list of what exactly they couldn't resist. Then pair the male and female students together and encourage them to have short, improvised conversations beginning: *Hello darling, I'm home. I just did a bit of shopping while I was out ...*

One or two pairs might want to perform their conversations for the class.

8 Talking Point

If students have just done the previous activity, choose only one or two of these points, which are rather similar, before moving on to the next activity.

9 Planning a party

The first part of this task is a ranking activity. You may want to give students some sentence starters for completing this, such as:

Well, for me personally, the most important thing is ... , because ...
What I like is ...
What I don't like is ...

The re-ordering of the jumbled conversation is a model of the kind of conversation they will have themselves in Exercise 10. The expressions to underline and focus on in this conversation are those which can easily be re-used and into which other key words can be substituted:

I'll bring some ... if you sort out the ...
How does that sound?
Well, to be honest, I'd rather organise the ... , if it's OK with you.
Couldn't you do the ... ?
Yeah, OK, no problem.
I'll try and bring some ...
What about the ... ?
Oh, I'll do that/those.
I'm looking forward to it already.

You might want to write these sentence frames on the board in the order they occur, to provide students with a model of the conversation you are going to ask them to have in the next activity.

The correct order of the conversation is:
a d c e b

10 Role play

This is a chance for students to recycle much of the language from 4a and 4b but it is also supposed to be a fun, interactive activity. To add to this mood, you may want to play some party music in the background while students are chatting and then circulating! As students are discussing the first five questions in pairs, encourage them to use some of the expressions from Exercise 9. The walkabout part of

the task also requires students to recycle the ways of turning down invitations given on page 62, which you might like to refer the class back to before asking them to try this stage of the task.

Workbook

14 Writing, page 31

11 Talking Point

After students have discussed the presents, ask them to have a look at the shop window and to see if they can name the objects or say what they are for. This is a great opportunity to practise language for describing things and their position:

What's that yellow thing that looks a bit like a ship?
(a butter dish)
What's that black thing with the orange circle?
(a lighter for a gas cooker)
What's that thing in front of it?
(an egg timer)

Ask a few questions like this and then encourage the students to ask you. Other objects include:

The orange thing in the middle is a sellotape dispenser. The thing behind it is a salad dressing set. The thing in front of the sellotape dispenser is a stapler. The silver thing on the right is an ashtray.

You could also encourage the use of *might* for guessing: *I'm not sure but it might be a spaghetti holder.*

12 Restaurant jokes (T27)

Ask students to cover the jokes so that they listen only. Play the first joke and see if they get it. If some do and some don't, get those that did to re-tell it to those who didn't. Then play it again but with students following the text this time. Do the same with the other two.

Vocabulary page

Do and make

1. make 2. make 3. do 4. made 5. made 6. do
7. made 8. make 9. do 10. make 11. do
12. do, make

The expressions are:

make a decision/make a noise/do the shopping/make money/made an appointment/won't do you any good/made a huge profit/to make an important phone call/do the washing-up/make your own way round to my place/do for a living/do something wrong/make mistakes

What a party!

1. birthday 2. house-warming 3. search 4. leader
5. farewell 6. political

Idioms

1. Long time no see! 2. Talk of the devil! 3. Beggars
can't be choosers! 4. Rather you than me! 5. There's
no time like the present! 6. You must be joking!
7. Long time no see! 8. no time like the present
9. Rather you than me! 10. Talk of the devil!
11. Beggars can't be choosers! 12. You must be
joking!

Verb + noun collocations

1. have 2. see, taking 3. got 4. give
5. tell 6. stand 7. set

Extra workbook exercises

11 Time and money, page 30
12 Expressions with *give*, page 31
15 Verb + preposition, page 32

Review: Units 3 and 4

1 Tenses

1. hadn't 2. I'd 3. I'm meeting 4. I hadn't been
feeling 5. I'll 6. hadn't been 7. We're going 8. I were
9. Will you

2 Expressions

1c 2e 3f 4b 5d 6a

3 Multiple choice

1a 2b 3b 4a 5a 6a 7b 8a

4 Conversation

1a 2e 3g 4d 5h 6c 7f 8i 9b

5 Collocations

1e 2h 3f 4a 5j 6d 7c 8b 9g 10i

6 Idioms

1e 2f 3a 4b 5h 6d 7c 8g

7 Real English

1e 2b 3a 4f 5d 6c

8 Vocabulary quiz

1. It means you can't find them anywhere.
2. You hold a house-warming party – even in a flat or
a bedsit! 3. Yes, because you're not allowed to smoke
on board planes. 4. You just didn't do anything
special. 5. No, you'd be very annoyed about getting
fined – especially if you got fined £450 for two
cigarettes! 6. Yes. 7. An appointment. 8. If you paid
me. 9. Have dinner there. 10. You smoke too much.
11. If you *go shopping*, it's for fun things like clothes
or shoes or CDs or whatever. If you *do the shopping*,
you buy all the things you use every day – milk,
bread, sugar, and so on. 12. At the end. 13. It feels
like it takes forever. 14. Yes. 15. A political party –
it's a kind of organisation; the other two you can go
to and drink and socialise at. 16. Yes. 17. You go on
one. 18. A court. 19. It's small, warm, secure and
friendly-looking. 20. On a plane.

Unit 5a
Last night

Unit overview

Topic

Talking about what you did last night.

The dialogue

Lucy tells Rose about her night at the worst disco in town. Rose tells Lucy about her quiet night at home.

Language input

- Auxiliaries – *Did you? That sounds fun.*
- Collocations with *get* – *get a taxi, got wet* etc
- Did/ had / went – *I did a bit of shopping. I had a really great evening. I went round to a friend's place.*
- Asking for repetition – *You went where?*
- Emphasising – *I didn't get home until 3.*
- Linking ideas – *The music was so loud, I couldn't hear myself think.*

Two role plays

The language strip

Ask students to find expressions about enjoyable experiences and expressions which are about things they didn't or wouldn't enjoy.

1 Lifestyle (T28)

Before the class look at page 72, ask them to discuss in pairs the questions at the beginning of Exercise 1 – *What sort of lifestyle do you lead? Do you go out every evening or are you the stay-at-home type?*

Before students discuss in pairs which of 1-10 they do or never do, you may want to ask them to look back briefly at the Time Expressions on page 29. These will help them talk about how often they do the things in 1-10. You could also ask them to talk about whether or not they did any of these things last night.

Listening to T28 once should be enough, but when the class have decided which speaker is talking about which number in the list 1-10, you could ask the class to read the tapescript on page 170 as you play the tape again.

Answers

The first speaker went to the laundrette; the second went out for a walk around town; the third had a quiet night at home; the fourth went to her evening class.

2 What's the difference?

Let the class discuss their ideas in pairs before you go through the answers with the whole group.

Answers

1. *Good evening* is said to welcome people, particularly in fairly formal contexts. *Good night* is said as a way of saying goodbye at the end of an evening together.
2. *Isn't it a lovely evening?* is likely to refer to weather. *Isn't it a lovely night?* is very similar.
3. *What did you do yesterday evening?* and *What did you do last night?* are similar, but *yesterday evening* suggests a slightly earlier time than *last night*.
4. These two mean the same.
5. These are basically the same, but *met up with* is slightly more informal.
6. If you *met* an old friend, it suggests it was planned. If you *bumped into* an old friend, it suggests you met accidentally.
7. *I went for a walk around town* implies that you knew where you were going. *I wandered around town* sounds as if you didn't know where you were going, and were exploring the town.
8. *We went out for a drink* suggests a pleasant social occasion. *We went out drinking* suggests you drank far too much deliberately.
9. *I spent the evening at John's place* suggests that you went there for a social evening, maybe for dinner. *I spent the night at John's place* suggests you stayed overnight.
10. *We had a meal together* means in a restaurant or at home. *We went out for a meal together* definitely means to a restaurant.

Draw attention to the Real English note: *an early night and a late night.*

Workbook

15 Sleep and dreams, page 38
You may want to use this exercise to teach some simple idioms based on sleep and dreams at this point.

3 While you listen (T29)

You could lead into this listening by putting the class into groups of three or four, and ask them to pretend to be the people in the four pictures on page 72.

Tell them to choose what they did last night from one or two ideas on page 72. Explain that they are all flat-mates and are just having breakfast. Tell them to role-play the conversation they think these four might have about what they did last night. This will give them the chance to recycle some of the vocabulary from exercises 1 and 2, and lead in to the listening.

Alternatively, just ask the class to read the introduction and questions 1 and 2 and point out the title. You could then ask them – if appropriate – what they think the worst disco in **their** town is, if any of them went there last night, why it's so awful, etc. Then play the tape and ask the class to listen – without reading – for gist. Next, let them read the dialogue as you play the tape again. Then, in pairs, ask the students to fill in the first two or three gaps from memory before you play the tape again, this time with pauses so that they can check and fill in the missing words. Do this two or three gaps at a time until the end. Play the tape through one more time with students following the script. You may finally want students to read the dialogue, or parts of it, in pairs.

Answers

1. Rose did a bit of shopping on her way home, then cooked some Japanese noodles, did a bit of tidying-up, read a bit, watched a film and then went to bed.
   Lucy went out with some old friends that she hadn't seen for ages. They had a drink and something to eat, and then they had another drink and eventually ended up going to this terrible disco, 'Stardust', where Lucy got chatted up by a much, much younger guy. She then missed the last bus home and had to get a cab!
2. Rose went to bed after one. Lucy didn't get in until three, and must've gone to bed soon after!

Workbook

8 Had to, page 36
This use of *had to* comes from an example in the dialogue. Do it in class or set it for homework.

4 Talking Point

This provides a fun opportunity for students to connect the content of the listening to their own lives and experiences. You may need to explain what being 'chatted up' means!

Draw attention to the Real English notes. You could also point out that *I bet* is often used on its own as a way of agreeing or sympathising with the person we're talking to. For example:

It was really funny when I told him I was 35.
> Yeah, I bet! He probably couldn't believe it.

See if the class can write a dialogue like this in pairs.

It is sometimes falsely believed that *taxi* is British

English and *cab* is American English. In fact, both words are common in British English.

Workbook

4 I bet + auxiliary, page 34

5 Responding (T30) (G17)

Let the class read the examples first and ask any questions they may have. Then ask them to read the examples again and listen particularly to the intonation and the stress of the highlighted language.

Next, practise this language chorally and individually and then ask students in pairs to read the two mini-conversations, trying to copy the speakers on the tape.

Next, refer the class to G17 on page 182. Then tell the class to work individually for 1-8 first and to add the correct auxiliary questions and follow-up questions or comments. Check the answers and then put students in pairs to read the 8 mini-conversations. Encourage them to add another comment to make 3-line dialogues. Refer students to the examples in the blue box to show what you mean. For example, the first could be something like this:

I'm a pretty good cook, believe it or not.
> Are you? So when are you going to invite me round for dinner, then?
Oh, I don't know. Maybe sometime.

Answers

1. Are you? + g
2. Have you? + b
3. Did you? + d
4. Were you? + f
5. Are you? (or do you?) + e
6. Do you? + a
7. Would you? + h
8. Are you? + c

Talking about you

This gives students the chance to practise responding techniques in an inter-personal context. You could help the students by writing on the board five sentences using these starters that are true for you. Then ask students to write five true sentences of their own. Next, get the class to respond to each of your sentences using an auxiliary question and a follow-up. Finally, students walk around the class sharing their sentences and responding to each other.

Workbook

3 Responding with auxiliaries, page 34

6 Collocations with *get*

Tell students that *get* is one of the most commonly-used verbs in English, and ask them to go back to the conversation on page 73 to find and underline some examples (there are three: *got in late last night, get a cab, didn't get in until three*). Then brainstorm any other *get* expressions they can think of before doing the exercise.

Answers

1. my hair cut 2. money 3. a call 4. something to eat
5. upset 6. wet 7. surprise 8. a job 9. bus
10. lost

The *get*-expressions are:
I got my hair cut
I got some money from the cash machine
I got a call from ...
get something to eat
I got really upset
I got really wet
I got a real surprise
I've got a job
I had to get the last bus home
I ended up getting lost

Once students have personalised some of the expressions at the top of page 75, you could ask them which expressions can have *very* added to them. (You can't get *very better*, *very married* or *very pregnant*, but all the others are possible.)

To the four questions that close this exercise, you could add a few more, recycling some vocabulary from 1-10: *When was the last time you got a big surprise? got really upset? got your hair cut?* etc.

For homework, you could ask students to write a short story (about 100 words) called 'Last Night' in which they have to use eight expressions with get. It can be as strange as they like (forcing the use of these expressions means it will inevitably be a little strange anyway).

Workbook

6 Collocations – *have / get*, page 35

7 Did / had / went

This exercise focuses further on useful expressions containing three other very common verbs. You could begin by asking the class to go back to the conversation on page 73 and underline all the collocations using *did / had / went* that they can find. Then get them to try 1-20. As these are all very

commonly-used expressions, you might want to get students to say them several times after you have checked the answers.

When students are asking and answering the questions that close this exercise, encourage them to continue each conversation for as long as possible, by using the language from exercise 5.

Answers

1.	went	11.	did
2.	went	12.	did
3.	went	13.	had
4.	did	14.	went
5.	had	15.	did
6.	went, did	16.	had
7.	did	17.	had
8.	had	18.	went
9.	did	19.	did
10.	had	20.	went

The other collocations in the dialogue on page 73 are:
I went and met some old friends
We had a drink and a chat
We had something to eat
We had another drink
have a proper conversation
I just did a bit of shopping
I just did a bit of tidying-up

Workbook

1 Past simple 1, page 33
2 Past simple 2, page 33
The second of these reminds students that the past is often used when not actually referring to past time, such as with *wish* and *if only* and when wanting to be polite (*I just wanted to know if ...* etc).

8 Role play

Put students into groups of three if possible. Ask them to read the descriptions of the three people and then to look at 1-20 in exercise 7 and decide who might have done those things last night. Sometimes it could be all three, sometimes it's more likely to be only one.

Let them choose which person they want to be, and then role-play a conversation between the characters as friends having a coffee together. Encourage students to respond to each other's comments and develop the conversation as much as possible.

As a revision exercise in the next lesson, you could broaden the task and ask each student to choose as many expressions from Exercises 1, 2 and 6 and 7 as they feel are appropriate for the character they chose. Give five minutes' preparation time (this could be done for homework) before the groups then have conversations starting *Hi, how are you? What did you do last night?* Remember that repeating a task a day or two later usually results in improved performance.

9 You did what last night? (T31)

Before starting this exercise, ask the class how they feel when they don't understand something that someone is saying to them in an informal conversation, and how they deal with this lack of understanding – what do they say to the other person? Then tell them this exercise will help them develop natural, socially acceptable ways of asking for specific clarification of a word or expression they don't know, or didn't hear properly.

Students read the examples first, then read and listen, before practising the examples themselves in pairs, paying particular attention to how they say the questions in red.

Make sure students notice not just the clarifying questions, but also how these questions are answered. Point out how the first speaker answers by repeating the problem word and then explaining what it means.

Answers

Probable questions are:

1. It cost what? / It cost how much?
2. You had dinner where?
3. You did what last night?
4. You arrived here when?
5. You went what? / You did what?
6. It cost how much? / It cost what?
7. You found a (baby) what?
8. You went where?

With a multi-lingual class, a fun way of extending this exercise is to ask students to write three sentences about themselves using one word or phrase from their own language. This word can be a food, a drink, a thing, a place, a kind of building, etc. They then walk around class, telling each other their sentences, asking questions to clarify what the other person is talking about. For example:

In my country, we often have nasi goreng for breakfast.
*> You have **what** for breakfast?*
Nasi goreng. It's a kind of fried rice dish. It's really nice.

10 I didn't ... until ...! (G18)

Lucy uses the marked form, *I didn't get in until three*, to emphasise that this was later than usual. Let

students try 1-8 individually, and then work in pairs to justify their choices.

Answers

1b 2a 3a 4a 5b 6b 7a 8b

Discuss

Tell students to use *I didn't . . . until . . .* only if they feel it is appropriate. Ask them to try and develop the conversations as much as possible.

Workbook

5 Until, page 34

Make sure students notice in the Real English note that the plurals of *grand* and *quid* are *grand* and *quid*. There is no similar expression meaning *a hundred pounds*.

11 Linking ideas (G19) (T32)

Answers

1g 2e 3h 4c 5f 6a 7b 8d

This exercise focuses on a very common way of expressing cause and effect in spoken English. The examples in the exercise are typical expressions, so you could ask the class to try and learn all eight sentences by heart.

When they have finished the exercise, get them to cover a-h. Read 1 and see if they can remember how it ends. Let them look when they need to. Do the same with 2-8. Then, do the same thing in pairs. Begin the next class by repeating the task.

Another way of revising these expressions is to make dominoes, with the starters from 1-8 on the right-hand sides of the domino and the ending from a-h on the left. The first domino has a blank left-hand side, the last has a blank right.

The more expressions students learn, the more fluent they will become. It almost certainly improves their understanding of grammar over time as well.

More conversations

Let students generate their own ideas in pairs and accept their answers if they sound OK to you, but when rounding up the task you might want to point out that there are fairly predictable ways of ending most of these sentences too:

Possible endings are:

1. It was so bad, I walked out halfway through/after half an hour.
2. It was so delicious, I'm going to go back again tonight!/I ate more than I should have.

3. I was in bed by nine!/I just went straight to bed as soon as I got in.
4. it was so boring, I nearly fell asleep in the middle of it./I wish I hadn't gone at all.
5. I got so annoyed about everything, I couldn't tell him how I really feel about things./I just stormed out. I got so upset, I just burst into tears.
6. I was so nervous, I just messed the whole thing up/I couldn't concentrate.

Workbook

7 *So* and *such*, page 35

Photo opportunity

As a lead-in to the role play, ask students what they think is happening in this photo (page 77), what kind of questions the police might be asking, if anything like this has ever happened to any of them, what happened, etc.

12 Role play

This is a very light-hearted way of reviewing some of the language presented in this unit. Give the two suspects and the rest of the class between five and ten minutes to prepare their stories and questions. During the interviews, make a note of any vocabulary or grammar problems that arise. Round up the activity by writing these mistakes on the board and ask students to correct or improve them.

Unit 5b
Relationships

Unit overview

Topic

Relationships, describing what you like in a partner.

The text

A 17-year-old finds love with a 58-year-old woman.

Language input

- Using *look – He looks as if ... He looks like a ...*
- Descriptive adjectives: *warm, pushy, hairy*
- Expressions with modals – *You must be joking! I can't believe it! You must be mad. I could do with a ...*
- Stages of a relationship – *started going out with her, just got engaged, separated, getting divorced* etc

Reading text

Partner shopping – supermarkets which help you find a partner.

The language strip

Use these tasks or your own ideas to exploit the strip:
Find two expressions which are very strong, and which you could only use if you were very annoyed with the person you were speaking to.
Find expressions which express preferences. Do you have the same preferences?

Lead in

If you practised the linking expressions on page 77 in the previous lesson, ask students to do the practice again before beginning this unit. Remember that repeating an activity helps to fix language in students' long-term memories.

1 Judging by appearances (G20)

As the class are reading through the nine examples given, point out the Real English note, as it explains two items of vocabulary (*creep* and *nerd*). In pairs, students match the examples to whoever they feel deserves them!

When students are discussing which people in the photo appeal to them, encourage them to use *He/She looks ...* when they explain their preferences. You might want to write other expressions on the board: *She/He's not my type. She/He looks too ... for me. I quite fancy him/her.*

Answers

a. looks like b. looks c. looks as if

2 What turns you on?

You may need to point out that *partner* is now very commonly used to mean *my boyfriend/girlfriend/ husband/wife/fiancée* and is useful if you don't want the person you're talking to to know the exact nature of your relationship with this person.

Notice the rubric asks students to rank the ideas for a partner or a friend. Do the activity twice if you like – once for a partner and once for a best friend.

3 Prepositions

All the prepositions here are from prepositional phrases in the text. If the class finds the exercise hard, you may want to give the answers and check students understand the vocabulary before reading. If you do this, you could look at the seven prepositional phrases and the title of the text and ask students to predict as much as they can about what the text will be about.

Answers

1. to 2. of 3. with 4. in 5. for 6. of 7. with

Workbook

13/14 Expressions with *on*, page 37
Remind students that prepositions are best learned as part of expressions.

4 While reading

Make sure the class read the introduction and the three questions before reading, and give them a few minutes in pairs to discuss their answers once they have read the text. You may want to read the text aloud to the students as they follow in their books. Remember that listening and reading at the same time shows students how language is chunked, and correctly chunked language has more chance of being acquired.

Two other items of vocabulary that may need explaining in the text are *mates* and *lad*. Men, and particularly younger men, often talk about their *mates* to mean their friends. The phrase *a mate of mine* is also very common. *Lad* is commonly used in the north of England to mean 'young man'. It also has a more negative connotation. If you talk about *laddish behaviour* or *lad culture*, it means young, macho, sexist, aggressive, unruly and offensive.

Answers

1. Because she's so much older than he is – she's old enough to be his grandmother!
2. Jamie met Jane because she was working in

the cloakroom of a club he went to with his mates one night.
3. Really well.

5 Comprehension check

Ask students to try to answer 1-6 on their own without looking back at the text and then compare their answers with a partner. If there are differences, let them look back at the text to clear these problems up. When checking the answers, repeat the vocabulary in the text that helped students make their decisions – *he fell in love with someone old enough to be his grandmother, he tends to find them a little bit immature*, etc.

Answers

1. False – but his new girlfriend is old enough to be his grandmother.
2. True – he tends to find them a bit immature.
3. True – she caught his eye across the crowded dance floor, although she wasn't dancing, she was working!
4. True – she thought he was just some lad with a few too many beers inside him.
5. False – the article says they just couldn't believe it.
6. True – they even invite her over when Jamie's out somewhere else.

6 Word check

Put the class into pairs and give them two minutes to see if they can remember any of the missing words, and then another two to scan through the text. Give the paragraph references if you want to speed up this exercise a little.

Answers

1. divorcee (paragraph 2)
2. blossomed (paragraph 2)
3. cloakroom (paragraph 2)
4. appealing (paragraph 3)
5. lad (paragraph 4)
6. sensible (paragraph 4)

Workbook

16 Expressions with *break*, page 38
17 Phrasal verbs with *break*, page 38

Read the Real English note *I tend to find them ...* with the class. Then give them five minutes to write as many statements about their own habits and opinions using *tend to* as they can, and then ask them to compare their answers with a partner.

Alternatively, split the class into male/female groups and ask each group to write ten sentences about the differences between men and women – using *tend to* so as to avoid a war!

Give some topics to write about, such as clothes, money, relationships, sport etc. Then make pairs from the two groups to share their ideas.

7 Stages of a relationship

Point out the expressions with *get: getting married, just got engaged, getting divorced.*

If you have a multi-national class, you might want to talk about what *getting engaged* means in their culture: Do they exchange rings? How long is the engagement usually? Do people have engagement parties?

Answers

A possible order is: d, g, c, b, f, e, a, h.

8 Talking Point

Be sensitive to students' views and personal experiences when you discuss this kind of topic. Students are entitled not to join in discussions which make them feel uncomfortable.

If possible and appropriate, put the class in mixed-sex groups for this Talking Point. Give students a couple of minutes to read through all the questions and ask you about anything that is not clear to them before they discuss them in their groups. Tell students not to feel they have to answer all the questions and that they are free to ignore anything that they feel is too personal!

If the class enjoy discussing some of these questions, ask them to choose one and write their views for homework.

9 Descriptive adjectives

Answers

Adjectives describing character: warm, flirty, pushy, quiet, forward, down-to-earth, unpredictable
Adjectives describing appearance: muscular, dishy, plain, hairy, skinny
Adjectives which could describe both: sexy, macho, mature, cuddly

It is important that you stress the subjective nature of these – and, indeed, most – descriptive adjectives. There are no correct Positive/Negative answers here, though obviously certain words, like *pushy*, are more commonly used negatively, while others, like *dishy*,

are generally positive. It is perfectly possible that some students find the idea of *muscular, dishy* men a turn-off, while others go for *unpredictable, pushy, macho* guys! Point out the Real English note on *dishy*.

Ask students to explain why the words have positive or negative connotations for them.

When students are describing the people in the three photos, encourage them to use *He/She looks + adjective*, as in Exercise 1. Obviously, when describing people in the class, they won't need to use this as their opinions are based on knowledge of these people and not just on visual impressions.

An extension to this is to bring in some personal advertisements from the newspaper – *Tall, dark, handsome man in late twenties seeks large, cuddly, mature lady for friendship* etc. Look at a few together as a class and deal with any new words and expressions. Then ask students to write their own personal advertisement. Put them up on the wall at the end of class. Perhaps somebody will find their dream partner!

10 Chat-up lines

This exercise is a piece of light relief, but does also introduce students to what may be fairly culturally specific pick-up lines, and thus guards them against them in future! Many students may not realise, for example, that number 1 is a chat-up line as old as the hills and would immediately ring alarm bells in many native speakers' heads!

It may be both amusing and educational to put the class into male/female pairs when they compare the best/worst chat-up lines! Students could discuss which might be said by a female and which by a male.

You could ask students if anybody can suggest some good ways of telling someone you are not interested when they try to chat you up.

Having discussed the chat-up lines, but before turning over to page 82, brainstorm on the board all the typical places that people meet potential partners – at school, at work, in clubs or pubs, etc. Then ask the class in groups to discuss the pros and cons of each place as a place for finding romance! This leads nicely into the next activity.

Partner shopping

Remember that the texts are to stimulate interest and discussion rather than detailed comprehension.

Ask the class to look at the photo. Point out that supermarkets are an increasingly popular pick-up place in the UK. Ask them to think of why this might be and what you can learn about someone from watching them shop in a place like that. Then ask the class to read the text and see how accurate their predictions were.

11 Talking Point

This allows the students time to respond personally to the text and to connect it to their own experiences and opinions. You might want to expand the discussion to include other modern meeting techniques such as Lonely Hearts columns, phone chat-lines and so on.

Alternatively, you could ask students to jot down what they typically buy on a visit to the supermarket and then ask them to swap shopping lists with a partner and say what they feel their lists reveal about each other.

Some classes would enjoy creating a role play of a supermarket encounter. Ask students to write down and then act out a conversation they imagine might occur between two shoppers with bleepers.

12 Expressions with modals (G21)

Let students try 1-9 on their own, and then compare answers with a partner before you check them. Then ask the class to read G21 on page 183. Finally, ask them in pairs to try and complete the 9 expressions at the foot of the page without looking back at the exercise above. As these expressions are so common in spoken English, it is a good idea to ask learners to repeat them several times both chorally and individually until they sound natural.

Answers

1. could 2. can 3. should 4. must 5. must
6. could 7. couldn't 8. must 9. might

1. That must've 2. You can 3. You must
4. You must 5. I just couldn't 6. I could've
7. I could 8. You should've 9. might fly

Grammar in context

This is simply a recycling exercise designed to elicit some of the phrases in new contexts. Insist on fluent pronunciation of the expressions. You could then ask students in pairs to have two-line conversations, with one student using 1-5 as prompts and the other then adding the appropriate phrase.

With higher level classes, you could now ask pairs to write nine more mini-conversations using these nine expressions in context.

Answers

Probable answers are:
1. That must've been nice.
2. You should've known better (after what happened last time). *or* I could've told you that!
3. You can say that again! *or* I know. I could hardly hear myself think!
4. You can say that again *or* I know! I just couldn't believe it!
5. You must be joking! (It was rubbish.)

I could do with ...

The possible endings to this sentence starter are fairly limited and a-h cover the most useful and widely used.

Round up by writing the following on the board and ask students to tell each other in pairs which ones are true for them:

> I could do with a drink.
> I could do with a break.
> I could do with a haircut.
> I could do with some new clothes.

Encourage students to have short conversations like this:

> I could do with a drink.
> > Me too. Shall I go and get a couple of coffees?
> Yes, that'd be great. Thanks.

Answers

1d 2c 3e 4a 5h 6g 7f 8b

Workbook

Modal related exercises:
9 Managed to, page 36
10 Won't, page 36
11 Modal verb expressions, page 37

13 Your dream partner

While this is a light diversion, it also revisits typical uses of *would* and *must*. The sentences in the blue box are only suggestions and students should not be restricted by them. Encourage them to include other categories and information.

After students have compared their wish lists, the discussion of the four people pictured provides an opportunity to re-use the sentence starters from Exercise 1 on page 78 and the descriptive adjectives from Exercise 9 on page 81. Provide new vocabulary where appropriate. Phrases such as *She's not really my type; He looks a bit too . . . for me* and so on would be useful for students here. You could briefly present a few of these phrases by modelling the task for the class first, giving your own personal preferences and feelings about the people pictured. If the class enjoy this, why not suggest they look briefly through **the whole book** to find someone they really fancy!

A nice follow-up to this task is to put students in pairs and ask them to choose the two people pictured on page 84 that they think make the most likely-looking couple.

14 Why aren't you married?

You might also ask them to think of any other questions older people have asked them about their love lives and how they deal with these! Have, for example, any of them been asked (if they are married) when they're going to start having children?

Remind students to make use of the Expression Organiser on page 189.

Vocabulary

Most of the exercises on the vocabulary pages throughout *Innovations* can be done at home or in class. The first practice here, however, is best done in class as pairwork.

Problem words

a. if you have a *chat*, it's usually with a friend and it's about nothing in particular. Your boss or your parents or your teacher might have a *talk* with you, and it's usually about a problem that needs to be sorted out or because you've done something wrong.

b. If you *gossiped* about the boss, you talked about all the rumours you'd heard, who they're dating, how they treat people, who said what to them and when, and so on. If you *talk* about work, it suggests you discussed business, how things are going at work, and so on.

c. If you *do the washing-up*, you wash the dirty dishes. If you *do the washing*, you wash all your dirty clothes.

d. I *went* to a disco is just a fact about what you did last night. We *ended up going* to a disco suggests you'd been to lots of other places first, and that the disco was the end of a very long evening out!

e. If you *miss the last bus* home, you don't catch it, and then maybe have to get a cab home, or walk! If you *miss a person*, you spend a lot of time thinking about them and longing for the day they get home.

f. If you *go out after work*, you go for a drink or to the cinema or you meet up with some friends and go

out for dinner or something like that. If you *leave work*, you just leave the building where you work.

1. I had a talk with her.
2. I had a chat with her.
3. We talked about work.
4. We gossiped about the boss.
5. I did the washing.
6. I did the washing-up.
7. we ended up going to a disco.
8. I went to a disco.
9. I missed the last bus home.
10. I really missed her when she was in Spain.
11. I left work last night about 5.
12. I went out last night after work.

Compound adjectives

1c 2a 3d 4b/g 5f 6e 7h 8g/b

Those describing appearance are: smartly-dressed, curly-haired, good-looking
Those describing personality are: self-conscious, open-minded, self-confident, easy-going
The class can discuss whether *football-mad* refers to personality or something else!

1. football-mad 2. smartly-dressed 3. self-conscious
4. open-minded 5. self-confident 6. curly-haired
7. easy-going 8. good-looking

Supermarket vocabulary

1. dairy 2. soft 3. delicatessen 4. meat
5. toiletries 6. poultry

Extra workbook exercises

12 Adverbs, page 37

Unit 6a
Telling stories

Topic

Anecdotes and stories

The dialogue

Diane tells Cathy about the time her father didn't recognise her.

Language input

- Story-telling expressions – *So, anyway, go on, all of a sudden, eventually* etc.
- -ing clauses – *I was standing there, minding my own business.*
- Idiomatic language – *eats like a horse, memory like a sieve* etc
  My feet are killing me. I could murder a coffee.

Reading text

The woman with a spider in her ear.

Learning advice

Throughout *Innovations* the emphasis is on the ability to say whole expressions naturally as the main means to fluency. This page provides the opportunity to discuss this with the class.

You could ask students to put a tick next to anything they agree with on the page and a cross next to anything they disagree with and then discuss their reactions in the whole class.

The language strip

Ask students to sort the expressions into two groups, those used by the person telling the story and those used by the person listening.

Ask them to find three expressions for starting a story and one to help finish a story.

1 Every picture tells a story

The first page encourages students to familiarise themselves with general story-telling before moving on to the more anecdotal. Before you begin, collect on the board the necessary items of vocabulary from each picture (*ship, rocks, run aground, parachute, power lines, naked man, hurricane, destroyed* etc).

Put the students in pairs and ask them to choose one picture each to tell a short story. They can begin: *Last year / week I was …* . This will be the first attempt of many at telling a story in this unit so it does not matter how able they are at this point. By the end of the unit, students should be considerably better at it.

Walk round and listen to students, feeding in extra vocabulary where needed. Get students to tell their stories to a different partner at least one more time. The way you tell a story improves the more times you tell it. Finally, choose individual students with interesting stories to re-tell to the whole class.

After this activity, the students might be interested to know the real stories behind the pictures:

The shipwreck is of a fishing boat which ran aground on one of the Canary Islands.

Beside it is a picture of the devastation caused by Hurricane Andrew in Florida.

Next is the hang-glider [parachute?] who got caught on power lines in Sussex, England. He was rescued safely.

Finally, the naked man was a streaker in the UK. We do not know why he was streaking! You may wish to ask students if streaking is a common activity in their country.

Workbook

3 Sentence adverbs 2, page 39
This exercise relates to the photo of the ship on page 87. You could use this now or save it to consolidate the language in Telling a story (page 91).

2 While you listen (T33, cassette 2)

If there is no underground in your area, find out if students have ever travelled on one. If not, explain a little about it and introduce the words *change* and *carriage*.

Before playing the dialogue, see if students can explain the pun in the title. Then discuss the Real English expressions and see if students can predict the contents of Diane's story. Without reading the dialogue, students listen for the answers to questions 1 and 2. Let them discuss their answers in pairs.

Let them read the dialogue as you play the tape again. Then, in pairs, ask the students to fill in the first two or three gaps from memory, before playing the tape with pauses so that they can check and fill in the missing words. Do this two or three gaps at a time until the end. Play the tape through one more time with students following the script. You may want students to read the dialogue, or parts of it, in pairs.

Remember that the more students listen, the more chance they have of noticing how language is chunked – where native speakers pause and do not pause. There is particular practice of this later in the pronunciation exercise on page 92.

Answers

1. It happened sometime last year/about a year and a half ago, on the underground.
2. Diane's father didn't recognise her to begin with, but in the end she spoke to him and he finally recognised her.

Workbook

5 Shall I . . . or not? page 40
6 Have something done, page 40
These exercises relate to things that were said in the dialogue. Use them in class or for homework.

3 Talking Point

Check students know the meaning of *ignore*. This exercise is best done in small groups first, with each group voting on the best travel story from the last question to be told to the whole class.

4 Hairstyles

Some styles are represented by more than one picture.

After matching, students could use the photographs and do a ranking exercise (1 = favourite hairstyle, 8 = least favourite hairstyle) and then justify their answers in pairs. Teach the expression: *I quite like this one.*

Alternatively, students could suggest which hairstyles would suit other members of the class or you!

You could also have students say the expressions by getting them to cover the left half of page 89 and then ask individual students to respond with the corresponding hair expression when you call out a photograph number.

You might like to check the following common collocations before students answer the questions:

dye your hair   *bleach your hair blond*
have a perm   *have highlights*

For higher level groups: *Do you think your hairstyle says anything about your personality? Have you ever decided to change your hairstyle radically? Why did you do it?*

Answers

Spiky hair – picture 3
Curly hair – picture 2
Fringe – pictures 5 and 7
Dreadlocks – pictures 1 and 4
Dyed red hair – pictures 2 and 7
Pigtails – picture 5
Hair extensions – pictures 4 and 8
Short back and sides – pictures 3 and 6

5 Vocabulary

As a lead-in, refer students to the 'glancing and staring' extract from the dialogue and ask them what the difference is. See if anyone can 'perform' these ways of looking for the class. Do students think any of the people in the pictures 1-8 are *glancing*? (Perhaps number 8.)

You could also teach the following expressions:

I glanced around the room.
I couldn't stop staring at it.
Stop staring!

Ask students to check in their dictionaries for any unfamiliar words and then put them in sentences 1-9. Explain that *wink* can be used to signal that something is a secret or a joke. Ask if it means anything in the students' own cultures.

As a follow-up, ask students to work in pairs taking turns to mime some of the ways of looking in exercise 5 for each other to guess the word. Demonstrate for the class first.

Answers

1. stared, stared 2. peered 3. glanced 4. seen
5. watched 6. look 7. glared 8. caught sight of
9. winked

The best way to learn these words is to learn the expressions they're typically used with and to try and remember the typical situations they're used to refer to – who would do each of them when, looking at what, etc.

Workbook

12 Ways of walking, page 43

6 Story-telling expressions (T34)

This exercise presents some of the discourse markers commonly found in story-telling conversations. Let students fill in the gaps individually, and then give them time to compare their answers with a partner. Then play the dialogue twice to allow students to check their answers and become accustomed to listening for the discourse markers. Then let them do the matching exercise in pairs. After checking this, play the dialogue again, but this time pause after each discourse marker and let students practise saying the markers, paying careful attention to their intonation. Play the tape once more all the way through before students read the conversation in pairs.

Answers

The missing words are: Go on, Well, Really?, so, Anyway, You're joking!
1. Well 2. You're joking! 3. Really? 4. Go on
5. Anyway 6. So

7 Talking Point

Firstly, find out which students would have kept the money from the cash machine and who would have told the bank. This information can then be used to organise the class into pairs or groups containing opposing opinions to answer the rest of the questions, thus keeping the discussions interesting. When answering 1-4, make sure students are using *I'd* and *I wouldn't* for these hypothetical situations. The following expressions may be useful to present:

> *I'd keep it.*
> *I'd try and find who it belonged to.*
> *I'd return it.*
> *I'd return it if (there was a reward).*

Find out how much the class thinks is OK to keep, and at what amount it becomes 'stealing'.

8 Short stories

These are probably best done individually and then checked in pairs.

Answers

Story 1: 4, 3, 2, 1
Story 2: 2, 1, 4, 3
Story 3: 3, 1, 2, 4

Links

Story 1: Well, and then all of a sudden, but luckily
Story 2: I used to, one day, when suddenly, so, anyway
Story 3: Once, and she suddenly, and so in the end

Make sure students are aware that these are only parts of larger stories. When they have put the stories in order, you could ask them what the speaker might have said before telling the story – *Did I tell you about ...* , *Have I ever told you about ...* . These stories can then be turned into dialogues based on the conversation in activity 6 like this:

> *Did I ever tell you about ... ?*
> *> No, I don't think you did. Go on.*
> *Well, ...*

In groups of three, students should take turns retelling one story each, adding extra information if possible. Monitor students' use of the expressions from exercise 6.

9 Telling a story (G22)

This exercise focuses on the way that different groups of expressions are used at different stages of telling a story. It also provides story-telling practice using these expressions. Give students time to prepare their stories in note form before they do the exercise. This will allow them the opportunity to ask you for new vocabulary and expressions (students may not see the puncture in the final picture. Ask them to look more carefully!). You could look at G22 on page 183 before you look at the language in the blue box. It could also be a good idea to model the pronunciation and intonation of some of the expressions in the box before students do the exercise.

Students should tell their story to three different people. Explain that performance improves when you do the same thing again and again as we all frequently do when telling stories about things that have happened to us.

Workbook

2 Sentence adverbs 1, page 39
3 Sentence adverbs 2, page 39

10 Talking Point

As a break from anecdotes, this activity discusses news stories. A good approach would be to bring in some local newspapers to give to students to help them answer the questions in small groups. One person from each group reports their findings back to the class.

As a follow-up to this discussion, students could choose one of the story ideas from 1-6 and write a short article about it. First, in pairs students take turns being a reporter and the other person (the owner of the parrot, the footballer, the local boy or girl, the headmaster, the factory manager or a worker) and carry out short interviews. The notes from the interviews can then be the basis for the articles which could then be read by other students or collected and made into a class newspaper.

Workbook

If you haven't already used it, read the story in Finish the story, page 39 to inspire students to write something.

11 *-ing* clauses (G23)

This is a common structure found in story-telling. You could first write the example and two or three others containing two separate *-ing* clauses on the board and rub out the subject and auxiliary to show them how it works. Then let students read the Grammar Commentary on page 183 before doing the exercises. Check 1-12 before they go on and do the grammar activity.

Answers

The unnecessary words are:

1. He was 2. They were 3. It was 4. He was
5. I was 6. They were 7. She was 8. We were
9. They were 10. minding my own business.
11. passing through London on the underground.
12. thinking, *Who's this lunatic staring at me?*

Grammar activity

Possible answers

There was this really strange-looking guy, hanging around, talking to himself ...
I was rushing around madly, trying to pack my stuff, hoping I hadn't forgotten anything ...
On Thursday I was driving along, listening to the radio, singing along to this song ...
So there we were, in this fancy restaurant, trying to decide what to eat ...
My uncle was sitting there in the bar, drinking double whiskies, smoking like a chimney ...
There was this huge crowd outside the parliament building, waving placards and shouting slogans ...

Pronunciation (T35)

Separate bits of information are usually clearly identified for the listener by pauses. When students fail to do this, it can make comprehension difficult. Similarly, when students are speaking, if they pause too much or in the wrong places, they are more difficult to understand. Students need to learn where to pause and where not to pause. This is especially true when dealing with complex sentences containing many connected main clauses such as those in exercise 11. The pronunciation exercise practises this as well as making students aware of the stress on the – *ing* form of the verb.

Take your time with this activity as it is probably something students are unfamiliar with.

Answers

There was this great big <u>dog</u>, <u>si</u>tting there, <u>bar</u>king at me.

1. It was five or six o'<u>clock</u> and I was just <u>stan</u>ding there, <u>min</u>ding my own <u>bu</u>siness.
2. My <u>dad</u> was actually coming <u>back</u> from a <u>bu</u>siness trip ab<u>road</u>, <u>pa</u>ssing through <u>Lon</u>don.
3. He keeps on <u>glan</u>cing at me, <u>thin</u>king, "<u>Who's</u> this <u>lun</u>atic <u>sta</u>ring at me?"

4. I was <u>dan</u>cing about in the <u>street</u>, <u>ac</u>ting like a <u>fool</u>.
5. I was <u>ly</u>ing there on the <u>ground</u>, <u>scream</u>ing in <u>pain</u>.

Grammar check

This can be done in class or for homework.

Answers

1. waiting 2. minding 3. packing 4. doing
5. sunbathing 6. trying

Workbook

7 -*ing* clauses, page 41

Spider woman

Ask the class if they've ever heard of anyone putting an animal in a microwave or finding a mouse in a pie. It's likely that someone in the class will have heard of a 'friend of a friend' who has had a similar experience. Get this student to tell their story and see if the rest of the class believe them. Explain the idea of the 'tall story' or 'urban myth' (students will meet this again in the second part of this unit). Then let them read 'Spider woman' or you read it aloud while the class follow in their books. Do they believe it?

12 Talking Point

Check students are familiar with the names of the animals and insects first. Then get them to discuss in pairs. Afterwards, select individuals to give answers to the class. Check they are using the contracted *I'd* form to begin their answers. Find out why they give their particular response. For example:

> *Marie, what would you do if you found a mouse in your bedroom?*
> *> I'd scream.*
> *Why are you so scared of mice? They're harmless.*
> *> Well ...*

Find out if anyone in the class has ever found anything alive in some food or found a hideous insect in their room. Get them to tell their stories.

13 Idiomatic language

Comparisons

Show them the two examples before they complete the sentences. Model them and ask the students to say each of them chorally and individually several times.

You might need to explain the use of *goes like a bomb* as a common idiom to apply to a car that *goes very fast*.

The questions after the exercise encourage personalisation of the language.

Answers

1g 2d 3e 4f 5b 6a 7h 8c

If you've *got a memory like a sieve*, you've got a very bad memory and forget things all the time.

If you *feel like a fish out of water* in a particular social situation, you feel very uncomfortable and out of place.

If you *spend money like water*, you spend a lot of it – quickly, and probably more than you can really afford to!

Exaggerating

These are all extremely common expressions, so practise them, highlighting stress and intonation.

Students could translate the whole expressions (not word-for-word) into their own language. This might result in an interesting discussion about the use of 'death words' in their own language or what is used instead.

Answers

1. dying 2. murder 3. killing 4. murder 5. died
6. died 7. death 8. die 9. murder

The literal meanings are:

1. I'd really like a coffee.
2. She's allowed to do all kinds of things that other people are not allowed to do.
3. My feet really hurt.
4. It's very difficult trying to get him to do things.
5. I was very surprised/shocked/pleased when he told me that!
6. I laughed a lot.
7. I'm really fed up with it.
8. I'd be really hurt/upset if anyone else found out.
9. If he does it again, I'll be really annoyed/I'll get really angry with him.

a7 b3 c1 d6 e5 f8 g2 h4 i9

Remind students that idioms are particularly difficult to use in a foreign language and they must be very careful if they use them. They will always need to check exactly how they are used with a teacher or a reliable native speaker.

As usual, remind students to use the Expression Organiser on page 189.

Unit 6b
Difficult to believe

Unit overview

Topic

Urban myths and amazing stories.

The text

A boy runs away to Disneyland Paris with £10,000.

Language input

- Past simple / past continuous
- Vague language – *30 or 40 people, There was no hot water or anything.*

Reading text

Urban myths

Vocabulary page

The language strip

Ask students to divide the expressions into two groups:

a. those said by the person telling the story
b. those said as reactions by the person listening to the story

Then get them to find all the expressions which contain a modal auxiliary, and see if they can translate those expressions into their own language.

1 He used to be so nice!

Use the photograph to start the unit. Ask students where this photo was taken and what these boys (lads) might have been up to.

You might want to teach: *just hanging out at the shopping centre.*

Notice the boy on the right is holding the remains of a hamburger. Ask the class if anyone can work out the last place they were in the shopping centre. Then ask why young people hang out in places like McDonalds.

You could then ask the students what sort of things they get or got up to with their friends. Do/Did they ever get into any trouble? Then do activity 1 together.

Remind students about the common negative *used to* expression *I never used to ...* , which is more common in this context than *I didn't use to ...* . The expression *I know this boy / girl who ...* will also be useful.

2 Collocations

This pre-reading activity contains adjective-noun (*magnetic attraction*) and noun-noun collocations (*credit card*) which appear in the text. Take this opportunity to remind students how important it is to record such collocations in their notebooks.

Answers

1d 2a 3g 4f 5h 6b 7e 8c

3 While reading

Before students read the text, ask if they can work out what the story is about by reading the title. They should know *spree* from the last exercise. After they have read, they should discuss the comprehension questions in pairs before you check them with the class. Check that students understand the meaning of *£10,000 in cash* in paragraph 4. Give some other ways this word is used:

Can I pay cash?
Are you paying cash?
Where's the nearest cash machine?
I've run out of cash.

Answers

1. No-one – he went on his own.
2. He spent his time treating other kids to free rides in the chauffeur-driven car he'd hired, staying in a big hotel and, presumably, going on rides.
3. It ended when one of the security guards at Euro Disney notified the police about Lamine's eccentric behaviour.

4 Comprehension check

As usual, give students five minutes to decide on their own answers. Then ask them to compare answers in pairs before you check them. Ask why they think the statements are true or false, as this encourages reference to key vocabulary in the text.

Answers

1. False – but his story is a bit like something out of a blockbuster movie!
2. True – he spent over £7000!
3. False – he went round in a chauffeur-driven car.
4. False – it was a security guard who notified the police!
5. False – it was Peter Kerry who stole his dad's passport.
6. False – he's a serial runaway.
7. True – they'd left about £10,000 cash around the house.

5 Word check

Ask a few personalised questions to reinforce the target vocabulary. For example: *Have you been on a spending spree recently? What did you buy? Do you have a credit card or do you prefer to pay for things in cash? Why? Have you ever hired a car? What sort?*

Answers

1. spree 2. credit card 3. serial 4. cash 5. hired

Workbook

4 Cash and banks, page 40

6 Talking Point

Use these questions to stimulate a class discussion before students return to doing pairwork in the next exercise. You might need to explain the expression: *had so much money lying around.* A similar expression is: *He always leaves his clothes lying around.*

7 Role play

Once students have decided which role play they want to do, give them five minutes to plan what they will say. Encourage them to make notes but not to write a whole dialogue. Then get them to try the conversations. Monitor their performance. Then tell them they have two minutes to plan how to improve their conversations; you may have your own suggestions for particular pairs of students. Then get them to try the conversations again. If you are sure students will see the value in it, ask them to do the same thing once more, reminding them that repeating the same task will improve their performance.

Alternatively, if you have access to a language laboratory or a number of cassette recorders, it would be useful to record some or all of the students' conversations. The recordings could then be used for pronunciation or error correction (or just for fun) by replaying and modelling or correcting a few bits that are problematic. If you don't have these facilities, just select a few good conversations to be performed again in front of the class.

8 Past simple / continuous (G24)

In order to clarify the connection between this more formal grammar focus and the story-telling theme of this and the previous unit, you might want to point out that these structures are commonly used together when telling stories or anecdotes. The first exercise implicitly introduces the simple/continuous distinction through a simple matching exercise.

The co-texts will help students at this stage and they shouldn't have to refer to the structures themselves until they have to underline the verb forms at the end of the exercise.

Answers

1d 2a 3b 4c 5h 6g 7e 8f

The past tense verb forms are:
1. was just sitting, started 2. was leaving, remembered 3. was raining, was leaving, grabbed 4. was living, were happening 5. was just going, rang, was going 6. went, came 7. were trying, won 8. resigned, found

Grammar discussion

Students are asked to consider the meaning and use of the structures by discussing their appropriacy in slightly different contexts. For example, students will probably guess that 1a sounds wrong and can probably suggest that this is because you can only find a diamond once, while 1b sounds OK because 'many problems continued to be found in the system'. At this stage you might want to use a time-line diagram to help students who are having difficulty.

Answers

The wrong sentences are:
1a. *Finding a single diamond* does not happen over a period of time.
2b. *Getting stopped* by the police does not happen over a period of time.
3b. *Coming home on the tube* should be expressed as a continuous action – an extended period of time – as it is the background to seeing the old friend.

In 1b the speaker suggests that the problems were being found over a period of time while in 1c there is no suggestion of a period of time. Perhaps the problems were found on one occasion.
In 2a *got stopped* is expressed as one complete action. In 2c *getting tired* is expressed as happening over a period of time.
In 3a *I was coming home* expresses that the journey was in progress. In 3c *I came home* on the tube is seen and expressed as a single action with no reference to duration.

Once they have finished this exercise, students should read the Grammar Introduction section *Grammar – the verb* (page 176) for consolidation of their understanding of simple and continuous forms, before referring to G24 on page 183.

Grammar check

This could be done in class or for homework.

Answers

1. broke down 2. was walking 3. saw 4. were walking 5. was thinking 6. came 7. found out 8. was boiling

For the question at the end (*What were you doing when the clock struck 12 on 31st December 1999?*), you could ask students to create a list with the names of their classmates on one side and a space to write what they were doing beside it. Students mingle and find out what each person in the class was doing at the end of the last century and write it down. Check students are using the past continuous form in their answers. (The photo was taken in the centre of Brighton at midnight on Millennium Eve.)

You can extend this further by asking students to think of another significant event which happened in their lifetime. They could ask other students: *What were you doing when ... ?*

Workbook

8 Past simple and continuous, page 41
9 Conjunctions (*while, during, for*), page 42

9 Tall stories

First, see if students can recall what a 'tall story' or an 'urban myth' is. Then divide the class into four groups and select one story for each group to read and try to remember so they can re-tell it later. Students should use dictionaries for unfamiliar vocabulary. Then form new groups with one member from each of the groups of four. Students try to re-tell their tall stories to the others in their new group without the help of the book. Tell the class that only one of the stories is definitely true. They then discuss which one they think it is.

As an alternative, read the stories aloud to the class, after which students can discuss as a class or in small groups if they think they really happened or not.

(Of the four stories the one about the flying cow is definitely true!)

Point out the pun in the title *What a rat!* and *water rat*. Is 'punning' common in their language?

If students have internet access, ask them to search for more urban myths on the web. Ask them to bring any stories they think are interesting to class to put on the wall or noticeboard for others to read.

10 Being vague

Sometimes you either can't, or don't want, to be precise. This activity presents the precise language patterns which allow us to be vague.

Answers

Different techniques

1b 2b 3b 4b 5b 6b 7a 8a

... or something / ... or anything (G25)

Refer students to the Grammar Commentary.

1. a bit of wire or something 2. showers or anything
3. a hammer or something 4. or something like that
5. food or anything

-ish

1. sixty-ish 2. yellow-ish 3. seven-ish
4. purple-ish 5. long-ish 6. tall-ish

As an extra exercise, students could describe some of the photos in this unit and elsewhere in the book using vague language. Look at page 93 together and ask:

Is the woman smiling? (Well, sort of smiling.)
What's the man using to look in her ear? (a sort of torch thing.)
What colour is the man's hair? (It's sort of brown and greyish.)

Ask similar questions about the people on page 89. Ask about the colour of page 149 and so on.

Workbook

14 Vague language, page 44

11 Stories, tales and myths

Folk stories or fairy tales often have many cross-cultural similarities. Begin this exercise by seeing if students can match the pictures to the stories. Then see how the names of the stories are translated into English from different cultures. Next put the students in pairs to discuss the remaining two questions. Often the details of these stories vary from country to country. Finally, select a few students to tell their versions to the class.

It is vital for students to read extensively if they really want to improve their English. If you have any of these stories at home, bring them in for students to borrow. As these stories are written for children, the language is not too complicated and would, therefore, be suitable for the students to read in class or at home. The fact that they are already familiar with the stories will make comprehension easier and reading in another language more enjoyable.

12 The birds and the bees! (T36)

This joke only makes sense if students know the meaning of 'the birds and the bees' (the explanation of sex and sexual reproduction) and the use of the expression *Where do I come from?* which all children ask their parents sooner or later. You could explain this first so that students understand the joke on the first listening. Alternatively, don't explain anything and see if students can work out why it's funny.

If you haven't already done so, introduce the use of: *Do you get it (the joke)?* and *I don't get it.*

13 And finally

First give students time to prepare or even make notes for their stories.

Ask them to look at the language points and expressions from Unit 6a and 6b, especially the story-telling expressions on pages 90 and 91, the *-ing* clauses on page 92 and the vague language on page 99. Students should also do the translation exercises on page 189 before attempting this exercise.

Vocabulary

Trip, tour, travel etc

1. flight 2. journey 3. travel 4. travelling 5. trip
6. trip 7. travel 8. travelling 9. trip 10. tour
11. journey 12. tour

Different kinds of stories

1. love 2. hard-luck 3. old 4. bedtime 5. inside
6. tall

Slang

1c 2f 3e 4b 5d 6g 7h 8a

Phrasal verbs with *get* 1

1b 2a 3c
4. I'll get round to it sooner or later.
5. Can we get together to discuss it?
6. I'm getting behind with my work.

Phrasal verbs with *get* 2

1c 2a 3b
4. Right. Let's get down to business. 5. I didn't get in until 3am. 6. I get on really well with her.

Extra workbook exercises

10 Train vocabulary, page 42
11 *Some* and *any*, page 43
13 Expressions with *take*, page 44
15 Vocabulary – odd one out, page 44

Review: Units 5 and 6

1 Tenses

1. That must've been 2. I broke 3. I left 4. came up, started 5. I was cooking, didn't answer 6. I was watching, went 7. Were you living, died 8. I didn't arrive

2 Multiple choice

1b 2b 3a 4b 5b 6b 7a 8b

3 Expressions

1e 2f 3d 4c 5b 6a

4 Collocations

1. smoke 2. bump 3. mind 4. glance 5. feel 6. get 7. go 8. do 9. spend 10. catch up

5 Conversation

1a 2j 3d 4c 5h 6f 7b 8e 9i 10g

6 Real English

1c 2d 3g 4a 5f 6e 7h 8b

7 Idioms

1f 2a 3h 4g 5b 6e 7d 8c

8 Vocabulary quiz

1. Glare at them. 2. You go on one. 3. Someone who's able to make good decisions. 4. It could mean you're just going out for a drink or dinner with them, or that you're now boyfriend and girlfriend. 5. No! It just means that you accidentally meet them. 6. You go *to* one (but you go *on* rides there). 7. Someone who's already divorced. 8. You ask *Will you marry me?* 9. None. 10. You've sold it. 11. You fall asleep. 12. You do the washing. 13. No, they are attracted to you. 14. One that you found too personal! 15. A serial killer. 16. You surf the net. 17. They're young men. 18. A kind of film. 19. The cloakroom. 20. You like them.

Unit 7a
Old friends

Unit overview

Topic

Meeting people and catching up on news.

The dialogue

Barry and Sharon catch up with each other's news.

Language input

- Expressions with *point – I can't see the point. It's not one of my strong points.*
- Past simple / present perfect
- Present perfect continuous
- Time and reason adverbials
- Remembering – *That reminds me. I've been meaning to see that myself.*
- Adding comments with relative clauses – *I went to a friend's wedding last week, which was nice.*

Reading text

A Frenchman who windsurfed to England.

The language strip

Ask students to sort the expressions into the following groups:

a. those used near the beginning of a conversation
b. those used in the middle of the conversation
c. those used near the end of the conversation

Lead in

Ask students to look at the language strip at the top of page 104. Would the expressions be used to people we meet regularly or friends we haven't seen for a long time?

Alternatively, start the unit by asking students the first two questions of activity 2:

Who is your oldest friend? When did you first meet?

Tell the class who your own oldest friend is, then put them in pairs to answer the questions together.

1 Ten questions

Make sure students understand the idea of a formal reunion of old friends. For older groups, ask if anyone has been to one. If so, ask them to describe what it was like. Did they like it? What sort of things did they talk about? Had people changed? Were there any major shocks?

The expressions should not present any vocabulary problems but you should focus on their pronunciation. Model and practise them as whole expressions, paying particular attention to intonation and stress. As they are usually said excitedly to a person that the speaker hasn't seen for a long time, they are likely to have a wider intonation range than usual.

Ask the students to suggest some other ways they might finish the expressions in number 9. For example:

Are you still going out with John?
Do you still go to church?
Are you still really into music?
Do you still live in London?
Do you still play in a band?

Once students have worked out responses to as many of the questions and comments as possible, get them to mingle as if they were at an actual reunion, asking questions and making comments to the people they come across. You might also want to point out that the expressions are not all questions. However 2, 3 and 4 still anticipate some sort of response, as if they were questions.

2 I haven't seen you for ages

These are best done as pairwork. The prepared opening conversations for the photos should be kept brief. While the students are writing, move around the class checking work, helping with vocabulary and correcting expressions where necessary. Then let the students practise performing these a number of times before you select some to be performed again in front of the class.

3 While you listen (T37)

Check the students understand the following before they read the introduction to the listening.

I bumped into John the other day.
I caught up with the latest news.

Also explain the title expression: *Long time, no see.* Then without reading the dialogue, students listen for the answers to questions 1 and 2. Let them discuss their answers in pairs. Then let them read the dialogue as you play the tape again. In pairs, ask the students to fill in the first two or three gaps from memory before playing the tape with pauses so that they can check and fill in the missing words. Do this two or three gaps at a time until the end. Play the tape through one more time with students following the script. You may want students to read the dialogue, or parts of it, in pairs.

Answers

1. Barry's been working really long hours. He went to his grandmother's birthday party last weekend.
2. Sharon went to an art exhibition on Sunday, visited her friend Richard, did a bit of shopping at Camden market, and she's been doing things for college.

Draw students' attention to both the Real English notes. They might ask about the use of *actually* once they have come across it in the dialogue. Let them read the explanation and example and then write the following on the board and see if they can write responses using *Well, actually*:

1. *That party last night sounded really boring.*
2. *I suppose his children were really well-behaved.*
3. *What did you think of that book I gave you?*
4. *Is that English course you're doing any good?*

You could check this by choosing a student to read out statement 1 from above and choosing another student to reply. Do the same with number 2 etc.

Workbook
5 Ending a conversation, page 46

4 Talking Point

You say *'Yuk'* to indicate that you think something is disgusting or unpleasant. This question asks students to think of the type of things that they think are disgusting or unpleasant.

5 Pronunciation (T38)

Play the tape and ask students how the speaker sounds – sad, excited, surprised, bored? This should elicit 'excited', so ask students why. Demonstrate the intonation pattern and then practise it.

Then in pairs get students to practise saying 1 – 8 after the tape. Finally, in pairs, students could think of answers for 1-8 and take turns asking questions and giving replies. This is a good opportunity to practise the use of *Well, actually* responses. For example:

How are you? We haven't spoken for weeks.
> Well actually, I've been away for a couple of weeks.

6 Vocabulary

In this exercise, there are many expressions made up of simple words that students already know, but these often remain unused by students because they fail to notice and learn the whole expressions. Make sure students transfer these expressions into their notebooks at the end of the exercise.

Ask individual students to read whole sentences back to you as a way of checking answers, and at the same time you can check pronunciation and model the expressions for students to repeat after you. Then, where possible, use the language of the exercises to ask the students questions to consolidate their grasp of the expressions and collocations. For example:

Enrico, what would you say has been the high point in your life?
Claudia, do you think there is any point in learning grammar?
Carlos, you support Real Madrid, don't you? What do you think their strong points are? What about their weak points?

Answers

1. get 2. make 3. see 4. make 5. turning 6. strong
7. sore 8. high 9. there's no point 10. on the point of

7 Short negative answers

When students have matched the questions and answers, check them by asking individual students the questions. Ask all the questions several times until they can answer more automatically and with less reliance on reading the expressions.

When students do the translation part, tell them it is important to translate the whole expression and **not** the individual words. If you have a multi-national class, it can be quite useful here to pair or group students who speak the same language together. They could then cover up the English expressions and see if they can recall them using their own translations. In a mono-lingual class, this is even easier. You don't need to speak the students' language to do this type of translation exercise.

Answers

1C 2A 3B 4C 5A 6B

What's the question?

Choose a student to read out their statement 1 and another to reply. Do the same with number 2 and so on. As well as checking answers, this draws attention to questions and answers which frequently co-occur. For example:

What have you been doing recently?
> Not a lot. / Nothing special.

Possible answers

1. What've you been up to? 2. So, what was the film like? 3. How are you feeling now? 4. Do you see your parents much?

8 Talking about the past 1 (G26)

Past simple / present perfect

This grammar section focuses on these structures in the context of talking about the things you've been up to, either recently or over a longer period of time. The contextualisation of grammar in this way makes understanding easier and, hopefully, acquisition quicker.

Get students to attempt 1-8 in pairs without reading the Grammar Commentary. It checks their understanding of the way the present perfect connects the past to now. When they have finished, get them to read the Grammar Commentary on page 184 and see if they want to change any of their answers before you check them with the class. The examples in the Grammar Commentary should re-inforce the use of the present perfect – looking back on the past from the present.

Point out that a past time reference such as *last Sunday* or *ten years ago* refers to a definite time in the past and usually requires the use of the past simple as it is seen as finished or remote in time. A time expression like *for ten years* (as in the first matching exercise) is not specifically a past time reference and can be used with either the past simple or present perfect.

Answers

1b 2a 3b 4a 5a 6b 7a 8b

Grammar in context

1. stayed 2. 've started 3. went 4. stayed in, painted
5. moved 6. had 7. 've booked 8. went, saw
9. 've looked

This exercise consolidates the fact that the use of the past simple is linked to a past time expression. For higher level groups or students who finish early, ask them to discuss the difference between the following pairs.

1 a. *Did you see John this morning?*
   b. *Have you seen John this morning?*

2 a. *Did you manage to get to the bank today?*
   b. *Have you managed to get to the bank today?*

In 1a it is likely to be in the afternoon at the time of speaking, whereas in 1b it is still the morning. In 2a the banks are likely to be closed at the time of speaking, while in 2b they are probably still open.

Follow-up comments

Too often grammar exercises are isolated from context, thus obscuring their relevance to the real world. Keeping more context also exposes students to grammar patterns working together with other grammar patterns, which is what actually happens in real language use.

This exercise contextualises the sentences in 1-9 and develops the idea of the kind of follow-up comments that often follow a description of our recent activities. After students have had time to match the comments, check these as a class, selecting students to first read out the statement from Grammar in context followed by the appropriate follow-up comment from a – e. Then get students to practise these in pairs, making a short dialogue by adding a response, if possible. For example:

> *Guess what! I've started going to a gym. I'm really enjoying it. I feel a lot fitter than I did.*
> *> Well, you don't look any different.*

Answers

a9 b4 c2 d6 e3 f5 g8 h7 i1

Time Expressions

This consolidates the difficult area of whether a time expression refers to past finished time or a time that could connect to now. It also introduces the present perfect continuous, which is discussed in the next exercise.

Answers

1. a c e   2. b d f   3. a c f   4. b d e
Numbers 1 and 3 are the past simple.
Number 2 is the present perfect simple.
Number 4 is the present perfect continuous.

Workbook

1 Past simple / present perfect, page 45

9 Talking about the past 2 (G27)

This section explores the distinction between the present perfect and the present perfect continuous. The continuous is used to talk about what you've been up to recently. For example:

> *What have you been up to since I saw you last?*
> *> Not much. I've just been working a lot really.*

In pairs, get students to discuss whether they think a or b is more appropriate in the context given and why. Elicit a few answers from different students, but don't give anything away at this stage. Then ask them to read the Grammar Commentary on page 184 to see if they were correct. The correct answer is:

I've been waiting here for an hour – the speaker wants to stress the extended nature of the waiting.

The next example checks that students understand

that the present perfect continuous talks about an action extended over time. The correct version is:

I'm afraid I can't go. I've broken my arm.

Here the present perfect simple is best because although the past action is relevant now (the speaker can't go now) and thus needs a present perfect, the action of breaking an arm happens only once, not again and again. Therefore, the present perfect continuous is inappropriate in this context and the present perfect simple should be used.

As an extension, see if students can think of some other examples of actions that can't happen over an extended period of time. For example:

> *I've cut my finger.*
> *I've fallen over.*
> *I've won the Lottery.*
> *I've passed my exam.*

Now ask students to discuss examples 1 and 2.

You look as if you've been crying and *I've found your passport* are correct. Crying is always extended in time, but when you find something you have mislaid, it happens instantaneously. It cannot be extended in time.

Finally, it is important to note that it is not the meaning of the verb alone, but the whole context that decides whether the continuous aspect is used or not. *Find* can be used in the present perfect continuous in the following example:

> *We've been finding problems with the system all day.*

Workbook

2 Present perfect – simple or continuous, page 45

Adverbs with the present perfect

As this exercise returns to the present perfect, you might decide to do it after the Time Expressions on page 107. Alternatively, keep it for another lesson and use it as a revision exercise.

Although sometimes more than one answer is possible, the purpose of this exercise is to decide which is the most **probable**. Probable language – language which students are likely to meet again – is more valuable than possible language from an acquisition point of view.

Probable answers

1. never 2. just 3. almost 4. completely 5. almost
6. just 7. never 8. just 9. never 10. never

As an extension, you could ask students to work in pairs and create two-line dialogues based on sentences 2, 3, 4 and 6. For example:

I've just bumped into Harry on the tube.
> Really? How was he?

Workbook

6 Still, yet, already, page 47

10 Present perfect collocations

Certain words co-occur in predictable ways – *make a mistake*. It is also true that some words occur in particular grammatical patterns – *I haven't seen him for* (time expression). This exercise emphasises the way words and grammar co-occur in predictable ways.

For most of these examples there is no need to give rules, just ask students to notice and remember the patterns. You could explain that *the last three years* is a period of time, not a point in time, and is, therefore, used with *for* as traditional grammar books suggest. However, it is much more useful to teach expressions such as *for the past three years* as unanalysed chunks, in the same way you might teach *How are you?*

Answers

1. I've been at college for the past three years.
2. I've been travelling around Africa.
3. I've been studying to become a doctor.
4. I've been abroad studying.
5. I've been working as a volunteer in Africa.
6. I've been on a course to improve my English.
7. I've been away since Christmas.
8. I've been ill for the past fortnight.

Workbook

3 *For* and *since*, page 46

11 Grammar in use

As a lead-in write the three sentence starters in italics from 1-3 on the board and see if students can complete them using the photographs. For example:

Have you ever been to India?
Have you ever seen a cow lying at the side of the road?
Have you ever eaten a giant mushroom?
The two ladies are selling mushrooms at a market in Helsinki. Have you ever been to Finland?

Students can then write questions relevant to their own experiences as suggested. When they have finished this, they could mingle around the classroom asking each other these questions. Encourage students to respond to each other's questions by asking further questions to get more information or by offering more details about their own experience.

1066 all over again

Before students read the text, use the photo to check that they know what a *windsurfer* is (the person and the thing – the sport is *windsurfing*). You should also see if they know where the English Channel is and roughly how wide it is (about 20 miles at its narrowest point). Find out if anyone in the class has ever windsurfed, if they think it would be possible to cross the English Channel on a windsurfer, and how long it might take.

Before asking students to read the text, ask them why 1066 is an important date in English history.

After students have finished reading, ask them to complete these sentence starters about the text:

What amazed me was ...
What I found hard to believe was ...
Something that made me laugh was ...

Then ask students to tell the class what amazed or amused them.

An alternative way to lead into this text is to write: *windsurfer, English Channel, cigarette, return ticket* on the board and see if students can work out what the text is about. Students then read to see how accurate their guesses were.

Workbook

10 Past perfect, page 48
11 The French windsurfer, page 48 (more on the past perfect)
14 Windsurfing vocabulary, page 49

12 Talking Point

This is the follow-up to the reading. Students should discuss these questions in pairs or small groups. Then select a few individuals to give their responses to each question to the whole class. You will probably need to pre-teach the expression *put other people's lives at risk* and *ban* (verb and noun).

13 Adverbials (G28)

This exercise encourages students to offer more details about things they have done (*Why? How long for?*) in the form of adverbial phrases. This is essential for students to learn because without this skill, they have to rely on using simple, tense-based sentence grammar all the time. Compare:

I went to Brussels. I was there for a week because there was a big conference.
I went to Brussels for a week for a big conference.

Fluency depends on students knowing multi-word phrases which mean they do not have to construct complete sentences all the time.

The context of sentences 1-5 should suggest the answers. Students should read the brief Grammar Commentary on page 184 first.

Answers

1. for a few minutes to pick up some aspirins
2. just for a few hours to finish off some things
3. for a week for a big conference.
4. for the evening to have dinner with him and his family.
5. for the weekend for a friend's wedding.

It is important that the point of this activity is reinforced through the personalisation exercise at the end. Get students to write their three sentences first and while they are doing this, go round the class and check their statements, helping where necessary.

14 Oh, that reminds me! (T39)

Ask a student to read the example conversations with you. You take the part with the highlighted language. Practise the expressions in red before getting students to practise the conversations in pairs.

Then let students do the matching exercise before they hear the conversations on tape.

Answers

1d 2c 3f 4e 5b 6a

Although the conversations are full of useful expressions, the important ones for this exercise are:

a. *Oh, that reminds me. I must ...*
b. *I've been thinking about ... myself.*
c. *Oh, that reminds me. I must ...*
d. *I keep meaning to ... myself.*
e. *Oh, that reminds me. I must ...*
f. *Oh, I've been meaning to ...*

Workbook

16 Remind/remember, page 50

15 Pair work

This consolidates the last exercise and provides a chance for freer practice.

Sample conversation

I must remember to buy a birthday card for my brother.
> Oh, that reminds me, it's my dad's birthday next week and I still haven't got him a present.

16 Adding a comment (G29)

This exercise presents a traditional grammar point – relative clauses – but concentrates on two typical patterns – *which meant ...* and *which was ...* . Give students a few minutes to think of, or write down their comments and then select a few students to give answers to the class, correcting where necessary. Let students do the personalisation exercise in pairs.

Possible answers

1. which meant we stayed in the whole day.
2. which was fascinating.
3. which was really nice.
4. which was a first for me.
5. which meant I was about an hour late.
6. which meant I had to wait another year before I could apply to go to university.

Workbook

7 Adding a comment, page 47
8 Believe it or not, page 47

17 Talking Point

This finishes the unit by returning to the topic of old friends and reunions. Use it in a variety of ways:

1. Just read the information about the TV programme 'Surprise Surprise' and ask students to think of someone from their past they would like to meet again. They could then share their thoughts with a partner or in small groups, but be sensitive to the fact that this is very personal and could be uncomfortable for some. Do not force students to talk about things they would prefer to keep to themselves.

2. After reading the information about the TV programme, ask students in pairs which reunion story interests them most. This is simply a short reading task. (Check students understand *We just seemed to click* in the final story.)

3. If you use the idea above, it can be developed into a role play to practise some of the language in this unit. Give pairs of students five or ten minutes to decide the kind of things that could or would be said in their chosen reunion before trying the conversation together. One or two conversations could be performed for the class.

4. For homework, ask students to write their own 'story' like the ones in this activity, explaining who they would like to meet again and why.

Alternatively, ask them to write the conversation they imagine they would have once they are reunited with the old friend of their choice.

Unit 7b
Art

Unit Overview

Topic

Describing works of art, the purpose of art, and recommending things you have seen, etc.

The text

A controversial art exhibition.

Language input

- Expressions for recommending – *It's well worth a visit. It's OK if you're into that kind of thing.*
- Vocabulary for describing paintings – *landscape, abstract, still life*

Vocabulary page

The language strip

Ask students to find expressions they might use when actually looking at a work of art.

Ask students to find expressions which mean *I don't like it.*

1 Talking Point

It is probably best to adapt this exercise and ask the first four questions to the whole class in order to introduce the subject and to get a general idea of the interest the class as a whole has in art. For example:

Who goes to art exhibitions?
Vicki, what kind of exhibitions do you go to? What about you, Claude?

And does your home town have an art gallery?
So, when was the last time you went to it? What did you see there?

Who else regularly goes to exhibitions?

Then for the rest of the exercise ask students to discuss their answers in pairs. Complete this exercise by finding out who likes each of the two paintings and why.

The names of the major galleries:

London: Tate Britain, Tate Modern, the National Gallery, the National Portrait Gallery

Paris: Musée d'Orsay, the Louvre

New York: the National Gallery, Museum of Modern Art (MOMA), Guggenheim

St Petersburg: the Hermitage

Madrid: the Prado, the Reina Sofia

2 Before reading

Ask students to look at the photo on page 113. See if anyone recognises the work of art or knows anything about Damien Hirst, the very successful British artist who created it. If so, ask them to tell the rest of the class a little about him and his work. If not, give a few details yourself.

Damien Hirst was probably the most talked about British artist of the 1990s. He was born in Bristol in 1965 and studied in London. He organised a very famous exhibition called 'Freeze' which launched the careers of a lot of young British artists. Their work is often very controversial. It caused particular controversy in New York, where the Mayor wanted the exhibition to be closed down.

Hirst's most famous work is called *The Physical Impossibility of Death in the Mind of Someone Living*. It consists of a giant dead tiger shark floating in a large tank of formaldehyde.

Have students do the vocabulary matching exercise.

Answers

1c 2e 3b 4d 5a 6g 7h 8f

After you have checked this, ask students which of these words might help describe the sheep artwork on page 113 (*suspend, container, controversial, pickled, formaldehyde*). Get students to look at the title and, bearing the vocabulary in mind, guess what the article is about. The students are then ready to begin reading.

Now tell them that Hirst often gives long titles to his works. Ask students to work in pairs and think of a title for his work on page 113. You could write these on the board and get students to choose the best one. Tell students that they will find the real title and an alternative in the article later.

3 Comprehension check

Students should do this by themselves and then check their answers with a partner.

Answers

1. true 2. false 3. true 4. true 5. false 6. false

You might want to do exercise 5, the Talking Point now. As people often have very strong opinions about this type of subject, it could develop into a heated discussion. Try and get students to justify any claims they make! Give students time to think about what they want to say. Two or three minutes silently considering a question before answering it makes a significant difference to students' performance. It also gives those with more reserved personalities the chance to get more involved, rather than having to listen to the more vocal students straightaway.

To help with the discussion, put some useful expressions on the board:

> Well, I totally disagree. I think (that art should be) ...
> I agree with that. I think that ...
> Well, I agree up to a point. I think that ...
> Art should be about ... not ...
> I prefer art that is about ...
> Hirst's work is awful / great, because ...

To finish, you could ask students to describe any other work of art they have seen recently that they consider shocking, or any work that is considered shocking by others, but that they really like.

4 Recommending (T40)

This exercise takes the art topic beyond just a discussion about art and introduces some useful phrases about going to exhibitions. You could lead into this exercise by asking why it is that when people travel, they often go to galleries in the places they visit, even though they might never go to such places in their own town or city.

Ask students what they would say if they want to recommend an exhibition they have just seen to a friend. Then get them to put the first conversation in the correct order and to find an expression for recommending (You should go and see it). Then they listen to the tape to check the order. Play the tape twice more before students practise the conversation in pairs, trying to copy the speakers' stress and intonation.

Answers

Conversation 1: 1e 2g 3f 4d 5c 6b 7a

Before listening to the second conversation, ask students what they would say if they wanted to recommend a friend **not** to go and see an exhibition. They then put the conversation into the correct order and find the expression for not recommending (I'd give it a miss if I were you.) Use the tape in the same way as with the first conversation.

Conversation 2: 1g 2c 3b 4f 5d 6a 7e

Recommending expressions (T41)

Let students reorder the expressions in pairs before you play the tape to check. Let them adjust their answers if necessary before you play the tape again, this time using the tape as a model to practise the expressions, paying particular attention to stress and intonation.

Answers

1. It's OK if you're into that sort of thing.
2. It's a must.
3. I really recommend it.
4. I'd give it a miss if I were you.
5. It's well worth a visit.
6. It's not worth the entrance fee.
7. It's not really my cup of tea / It's not my cup of tea, really.

2, 3, 5, are recommending; 1, 4, 6, 7 are not.

Get students to think of a recent exhibition they have been to and whether they'd recommend it or not. In pairs they should have a conversation with their partner using language from the previous exercises. They should begin with one of the following:

> I went and saw an exhibition called ... the other day.
> I went and saw an exhibition about ... the other day.

5 Talking Point

See 3 Comprehension check above for details.

6 Pronunciation (T42)

Play the tape of the example and see if students can hear the differences in the way *the* is pronounced.

Write *the National Gallery* and *the other day* next to each other on the board and get students to say both. Ask students to do the exercise. Use the tape to model the pronunciation.

Workbook

15 *The* or no *the*, page 50 (an exercise and a language note)

7 Vocabulary

If you have any postcards of paintings, bring them in for students to describe using this vocabulary. Point out that *portrait*, *landscape* and *still life* are nouns and the other words are adjectives.

Answers

1g 2c 3a 4e 5b 6f 7h 8d

For higher level classes, you could see if they can add to the list. Here are some further ideas:

> *ambiguous, avant-garde, boring, challenging, clichéd, decorative, dramatic, energetic, expressive, figurative, grotesque, intense, large-scale (small-scale), romantic, striking, subtle, symmetrical, vibrant, witty*

At this point you might want to ask students to do the vocabulary exercise on art movements on page 117.

8 Talking Point

Some useful disagreeing expressions for this exercise:

No, I don't think it's (traditional, a portrait) at all. It's more (abstract, like a landscape).
I disagree. It looks more (like a landscape, colourful) to me.

If you have brought postcards of paintings, lay them out on a table. Put students in pairs. One student from each pair comes to the table, chooses a painting and returns to describe it to the partner using three adjectives from those in the coursebook and/or the compiled list. The other student listens to the description and then comes to look at the paintings to try and identify the one which was described. He/She then returns to check. The language used to check will be useful 'identifying' language: *Was it the landscape one, the one with a man and a dog, the one with the snow?* They then reverse roles.

You could ask students to bring examples of their favourite work of art to class the following day and talk about the work and why they like it. This could be done in small groups or in front of the class.

9 Talking Point

This activity reinforces a lot of the language presented in this unit. It is better done in small groups. You might need to provide language such as:

I think it's disgusting / outrageous / terrible / offensive.
It doesn't really worry / shock / annoy / bother me.

Photo opportunity

This is a photograph of a wall beside a main road in Barcelona. You could discuss whether this is art or just graffiti. Is it wrong to paint on public property, even if it is extremely artistic? When is it OK? When is it not OK?

10 Art joke (T43)

Students can either guess how the joke ends by reading it or you can pause the tape just before the ending. Play the tape several times and pause to give students time to repeat parts of the joke and mark where the speaker pauses. Students can practise telling it to their partners, doing their best to copy the tape.

Vocabulary page

These exercises can be done in class or for homework.

Relationships

a. my next-door neighbour b. a chance acquaintance
c. a close friend d. a distant relative

1. next-door neighbour 2. distant relative
3. close friends 4. a chance acquaintance

Phrasal verbs with *out*

1. sold 2. turned 3. worn 4. fell 5. tired 6. make
7. kicked 8. stands

Art movements

1. Impressionism – Claude Monet
2. Cubism – Pablo Picasso
3. Art Nouveau – Antonio Gaudi
4. Surrealism – Salvador Dali
5. The Renaissance – Leonardo da Vinci

Places of work

1e 2a 3d 4f 5g 6h 7c 8b

Expressions with *get*

1f 2b 3e 4d 5c 6h 7g 8a

Extra workbook exercises

4 Expressions with *for*, page 46
9 Vocabulary – adjective + preposition, page 48
12 Weather vocabulary, page 49
13 Weather idioms, page 49

Unit 8a
Describing things

Unit overview

Topic

Describing things.

The dialogue

Paul and Mick discuss films they have seen recently.

Language input

- Negative questions – *Didn't you think it was a bit boring?*
- Comparing – *It was a bit like skiing, only a lot more difficult.*
- *Must* for guessing – *That must be nice. That must've been nice.*
- Linked questions – *What's his house like? Is it big?*
- Conjunctions – *although, considering, in spite of*

Reading text

To be or not to be – some quotations from Shakespeare.

Learning advice

This is another chance to remind students of the importance of phrasal vocabulary and of the Expression Organiser at the back of the book.

Ask students who have been keeping vocabulary notebooks to show them to the rest of the class and discuss how they have organised them.

The language strip

Ask students to sort the expressions into three groups:

a. positive reactions
b. negative reactions
c. sarcastic or flippant comments

Ask students if there are any expressions which they would not use themselves. Why not?

1 So what was it like? (T44, T45)

By now students should be familiar with the expression *What was it like?* However, some students might confuse it with other *like*-expressions, such as *What does it look like?* Ask if anyone has recently seen a film, a play, a band or a new programme on television, or if they have recently finished reading a book. Ask what it was and then ask what it was like. If you do this a few times with different students, the responses will help you check their comprehension of

the question as well as provide a lead-in for the unit.

Next, introduce the new vocabulary in exercise 1. Point students towards the Real English definition of *over the top*, on page 120. Then use the tape to model the expressions. Ask students to mark the stress, then let them practise.

Answers

1. It was ho<u>rren</u>dous.
2. It was a bit <u>bland</u>.
3. It was <u>wonderful</u>.
4. It was a bit over the <u>top</u>.
5. It was nothing <u>special</u>.
6. It was very <u>ordinary</u>.
7. It was a bit disa<u>ppointing</u>.
8. It was <u>really</u> <u>brilliant</u>.

Notice that in the last example two words are stressed: *<u>really</u>* and *<u>brilliant</u>*.

Students should then attempt to answer 1, 2 and 3. When they have finished, let them listen to the tape to see if they were correct. This will also provide students with the opportunity of hearing the expressions in context.

Answers

1. A play or performance: wonderful, really brilliant
2. A bottle of expensive wine which wasn't very good: nothing special, very ordinary, a bit disappointing
3. Food which didn't really taste of anything: a bit bland

When describing the pictures, encourage students to be imaginative and to put the expressions in a conversational context as in the last tapescript. For example:

I was stuck in this traffic jam yesterday. It was horrendous. It took me five hours to get home.
> Five hours? What a nightmare!

Look at those legs up there. That's a bit over the top, isn't it?
> They look brilliant. I love it.

Then see if they can come up with any other ways to describe either a traffic jam, an old cinema or even a film. Ask students to describe the worst traffic jam they have been in, a building that impressed them, or a film they have seen recently.

The traffic jam in the picture is on a section of British motorway famous for delays. The legs on top of the cinema are a well-known landmark in Brighton – on top of the Duke of York's cinema.

Workbook

1 Taste, smell, feel, page 51
2 Opposites, page 51

2 While you listen (T46)

Check that students understand the question: *What do they think of them?* Explain that it is similar in meaning to: *What was it like?* You could get them to write down a list of other questions with similar meanings in their notebooks. For example:

> *What was it like?*
> *What did you think of it?*
> *How was it?*
> *Did you enjoy it?*
> *Was it any good?*

As mentioned above, this is a good time to raise the issue of storing new vocabulary, as outlined on page 118.

Set the scene for the dialogue. As usual, tell the class not to try to understand every word but only try to answer the two questions. We suggest the text is covered the first time you play the tape. Play the tape twice if necessary so that students can answer the questions. Check their answers.

Answers

1. Titanic and Bomb Alert 2.
2. Paul really liked Titanic, Mick thought it was a bit over the top. Mick really liked Bomb Alert 2, Paul hasn't seen it – it's not his kind of thing.

Now see if they can fill in the first two or three gaps from memory with a partner. Play the tape again for students to fill in the missing words. Pause the tape so they have time to write in what they hear. Finally, play the tape again with students listening while reading the tapescript on pages 172-173. The missing words are highlighted in red. Don't be afraid to ask students to listen several times. The more students listen to natural spoken English, the more chance they have of acquiring that language and improving their performance.

Point students to the Real English note *It's not exactly Shakespeare.* Ask them to make similar statements for these situations:

> Describing a cheap, run down hotel:
> *It's not exactly the Hilton, is it?*
> Describing a battered old car:
> *It's not exactly a Rolls Royce, is it?*
> Someone who can't play tennis very well:
> *She's not exactly Martina Hingis, is she?*

Workbook

3 Expressions with *way*, page 51

3 Talking Point

This provides a follow-up for the listening. Students should answer the questions in pairs – make sure they justify their choices. Those who finish early should form new pairs and answer the questions again.

4 Negative questions (T47)

Get students to read through the introduction to this exercise. Then get students to change the following into a negative question:

> Do you want any of this pizza?
> *Don't you want any of this pizza?*

Ask students to explain why the speaker above might use the negative rather than the positive question (The first question is a kind of offer. The negative question expresses surprise that the other person has not eaten any of the pizza.) Students should then read the blue box, listen to this on tape and practise the three-line dialogues with a partner. Follow this with the Grammar in context.

Answers

1. Don't you find them hard to read?
2. Don't/Didn't you think she over-acted a bit?
3. don't/didn't you think it was a bit slow?
4. don't/didn't you think it was really romantic?
5. Didn't you find it quite funny though?
6. Didn't you find him a bit too much like Robert De Niro?
7. Don't you think it's a bit over-rated?
8. Don't/Didn't you think it was just silly and typical of late-night cable TV?

In the Grammar role play, encourage students to use the expressions in red. Remember to give students three or four minutes to prepare and ask them to repeat the task at least once, perhaps with a different partner.

Workbook

4 Negative questions, page 52

5 Talking Point

Model this pattern with all the adjectives and get students to repeat them after you before they do the exercise. Tell them they should briefly explain the plot of the film before they criticise it.

As a follow-up, you could list on the board all the films students have seen recently and discuss whether any of the seven adjectives describe them. If a film is described as violent, those who have seen it can then discuss whether it was a *bit too* violent or just *quite* violent etc. For a romantic film, some may say it was too romantic (really over the top) or just right. This could become an interesting class discussion as students' subjective views of the same film will differ.

6 Pronunciation (T48, cassette 2 side 2)

Use the tape as a model for students to practise the expressions, paying particular attention to the pronunciation of the contractions. Follow up by reading out the following statements and get students to choose which of the sentences from 1-12 would come next:

1. We were lucky that all he got in the accident was a broken arm. (It could've been very serious.)
2. I'm so sorry we sent you the wrong tickets. (There must've been a mistake.)
3. I'm so happy to hear that you won the neighbour of the year award. (It couldn't've happened to a nicer person.)

Get students to write similar first comments, as above, for expressions 2, 3 and 5 to make short dialogues.

Alternatively, let students choose which sentences to make statements for, and then ask them to read these to a partner who has to choose the right expression to respond with.

You may want to do this exercise, either just before or after exercise 8, *Must* for guessing.

7 Comparing (G30)

This activity goes beyond the traditional comparative (*A is bigger than B*) and introduces the natural comparatives used by fluent educated speakers.

Model the examples and get students to practise them, paying attention to pausing. For example:

Oh, all right I suppose. | It was a bit like last year's really | but not as good.

It is often students' inability to chunk language naturally and pause **between** groups of words (and **not** pause **within** those groups) that makes their spoken English difficult to understand.

The Grammar Commentary on page 184 draws attention to the use of *there's* as opposed to *there are* with plural nouns, as seen in some of the examples in this exercise. For more detailed commentary on the grammar of comparatives, refer students back to G3 on page 178.

Answers

1e 2g 3b 4a 5f 6h 7d 8c

When students have finished this exercise and answers have been checked, get them to practise the mini-conversations in pairs.

Then with the same partner they should take turns using the comparative expressions to describe the things in the pictures.

For the next exercise they should work alone to write descriptions of 1 - 8, before changing partners to do the last guessing exercise.

Workbook

All the exercises below practise other ways of comparing. Use them in class or give them for homework.
5 Easily the biggest, page 52
6 The best ever, page 52
7 Comparison, page 52

8 *Must* for guessing (G31)

Read the Grammar Commentary on page 184 with students and then read the examples in the box.

Read the first sentence of each example again and choose students to read the response with *must* as a way of practising the form and checking pronunciation.

Answers

Grammar check

1. must be 2. must be 3. must've been 4. must be
5. must be 6. must've been 7. must be 8. must be
9. must've been

Grammar in context

Possible answers

1. That must be hard work. 2. That must've been nice/horrible. 3. That must keep you fit. 4. It must've been beautiful. 5. That must be awful.
6. That must've been horrendous. 7. It must've been awful. 8. That must be nice.

Workbook

There are two jokes with *must've* on page 53. Ask the class to vote on their favourite. Give 8 Must've for homework.

9 Talking Point

Read out the example, then tell students about something interesting you've done or seen recently and try and elicit a few replies using *must've been*.

You might need to prompt this by writing *That must've been ...* , on the board. Then give students some time to write down their own interesting experiences before they talk about them in pairs. If students are lacking ideas, tell them to use the photos at the bottom of the page.

The photos are, from left to right: the Orissa region in eastern India, Venice, Loch Seaforth in the Outer Hebrides.

Alternatively, ask the class to guess where these places are, what they're like, using the following structures:

This must be ... (or ...) or somewhere like that.
It must be really / quite ... there.

You could extend this by asking what it must be like to live in one of the places.

To be or not to be

As a lead-in and to set up the reading, write *To be or not to be, that is the question,* on the board and ask students if they know where it comes from (*Hamlet* by Shakespeare). If anyone does know, ask if they can briefly summarise the story of Hamlet:

A king dies in suspicious circumstances. His widow starts an affair with her brother-in-law. Her son is jealous, suspicious and becomes very moody. His girlfriend thinks he doesn't love her any more, so she commits suicide. The son then kills his uncle. The mother commits suicide. At the end Hamlet is killed.

Get a few translations of *to be or not to be,* from the students' own language. Ask if they know any other quotations from Shakespeare. Ask them why they think quotations become famous (an answer is given in the text). Then let students read the text silently, or better still, you read the text aloud as they follow.

Put students into small teams to complete 1-8. Give points for guessing the correct answer. For higher level groups, you might like to discuss the meanings of some of the quotations together.

Answers

1. cruel 2. wicked 3. name 4. music 5. madness
6. gold 7. self 8. love

10 Talking Point

Put the students in pairs to answer these questions, then put two pairs together to check their answers as a group of four.

Answers

1. 1564 – 1616 2. Stratford-on-Avon 3. Anne

Hathaway 4. Othello, Macbeth, Merry Wives of Windsor 5. Romeo and Juliet (West Side Story)

11 Asking linked questions (T49)

Questions are often asked two at a time; particularly questions that ask for a description. The second question often presupposes the answer: *What's his house like? Is it big?* This exercise explores this area of spoken language.

As the exercise allows for a variety of answers, it is a good idea to go around the class checking and correcting as the students are writing. Let students compare their finished answers with their partner.

Possible answers

2. What was that book like? Was it interesting?
3. What's your new job like? Are you enjoying it?
4. What was Tunisia like? Was it warm?
5. What's this CD like? Is it any good?
6. How was the match? Did you win?

Pairwork

Before students do this exercise in pairs, you will need to check they are on the right track. Elicit possible questions for both a and b.

What was the weather like on your trip to Indonesia? Was it OK?
What's your job like? Is it interesting?

You might decide to start this exercise as a whole class. Choose one student to ask another for the first two or three questions so that everyone gets a clear idea of what to do before they complete the exercise in pairs.

Workbook

9 Linked questions, page 53

12 Conjunctions (G32)

The conjunctions *although, considering,* and *in spite of* often appear in conversations describing things. First, get students in pairs to try to work out the difference in meaning between the conjunctions from the examples. Then read the Grammar Commentary on page 185 together. Students should then do the gap-fill exercises.

Answers

1. Talking about a new CD:
a. considering b. although c. although d. considering
2. Talking about a trip:
a. although b. considering c. although d. considering
3. Talking about buying a watch:
a. although b. in spite of c. in spite of d. although

Workbook

10 *Considering* and *although,* page 54
11 In spite of, page 54
12 . . . though, page 54

Before students do the final speaking exercise at the bottom of page 125, quickly revisit some of the language discussed so far in this unit. In particular, look at the adjectives in exercise 1; *It's not exactly ... ,* in exercise 2; the expressions in exercises 5 and 7. They should also do the translations on page 190. Also, when students are writing their three questions, encourage them to use the kind of linked questions which they practised in exercise 11.

Unit 8b
Films and television

Unit overview

Topic

Films, TV and censorship.

The text

A film which was adapted for TV is criticised for not being violent enough.

Language input

- Film and TV vocabulary – *soundtrack, special effects, scene, series, remote control* etc
- Past perfect
- Expressions for talking about films – *I loved every minute of it. It's one of the best films I've ever seen.*
- Asking questions about films – *Who's in it? What's it about? Who's it by?*
- Saying you can't remember – *I can't remember off the top of my head. Wait. It'll come to me in a minute.*
- Contradicting – *Well, actually, I do.*

The language strip

Ask students which of the expressions relate to films, which to TV programmes, and which could be both. Ask them to find all the questions in the strip and think of one answer to each question.

In addition, you can ask students to look at the sentences and answer these questions:

What's the situation? Who is talking to who(m)? What about? What could be said in reply? How would you say this in your own language?

1 What kind of film is it?

Begin with a general class discussion prompted by the questions at the beginning of this exercise (use the photos from the films on pages 126 and 127). See if students recognise any of the actors.

The three films on page 126 are: *Four Weddings and a Funeral, Titanic,* and *Braveheart.* The main actors visible are Rowan Atkinson, Leonardo Di Caprio, Kate Winslet and Mel Gibson. The film on page 127 is *Henry the Fifth* with Kenneth Branagh.

Check students understand the six descriptions. A *weepie* is a film that makes you cry a lot, and if students are unsure of *a sci-fi thing* you could refer them to the photo from *Robocop* on page 128. Do the matching task in pairs but first teach the expression:

It's a cross between a (comedy) and (a sci-fi thing).

as some films obviously do not fit into simple categories.

Suggested answers

Four Weddings and a Funeral is a comedy.
Titanic is a real weepie.
Braveheart is a cross between a costume drama and an action movie.
Henry the Fifth is a costume drama.

When students have finished, put the six film categories in a row on the board and ask the class to suggest other films in those categories.

2 Film vocabulary

Students could use their dictionaries to do this exercise.

Answers

1. director 2. banned 3. stars 4. special effects
5. cut 6. dubbed 7. dialogue 8. soundtrack
9. plot 10. ending 11. set 12. scene

Workbook

14 At the cinema, page 55

3 Talking Point

These questions provide a personalised follow-up to exercise 2 and consolidate the meaning of the new vocabulary. Do it in pairs or small groups. Some further questions you might get students to answer are:

a. Do you know of any films that have been banned in your country? Why? Do you agree with the decision?

b. Do you ever go and see a film just because it stars your favourite actor/actress or because it is by your favourite director?

c. Who's your favourite director or actor/actress? Why?

d. How important is the plot of a film to you? Can you think of a film that initially had a great plot, but was let down by the ending?

4 Before you read

Begin by referring students to the photo from *Robocop* on page 128. See if anyone recognises this science fiction film about a prototype law-enforcing robot that goes out of control and causes havoc. ('Robo' from robot and 'cop' from copper – English slang for policeman.) Ask if they liked it or not and whether they thought it was very violent. Explain that the article is about the film itself and its violent nature. Then ask students to do the vocabulary exercise, using dictionaries where necessary.

Answers

1h 2e 3j 4i 5f 6g 7a 8d 9b 10c

After checking the answers, spend a few minutes asking the whole class the questions below the exercise.

5 While reading

Tell the class that when *Robocop* was shown on TV, there were a lot of complaints from viewers. Ask the students to read the text to find out why. After checking briefly, ask students to answer questions 2, 3 and 4 in pairs.

Answers

1. Because too much violence had been cut.
2. It ruined the film.
3. Michael Winner was *Robocop's* director. He was pleased people complained.
4. Mary Whitehouse represents the National Viewers' and Listeners' Association. She feels people should be able to give up bits of film in order to reduce the amount of violence on TV.

Real English

Bad language or swear words are often avoided in English courses, but are common in real-life conversation. However, with the increasing incidence of swear words in films, newspapers and even on BBC television, which is renowned for high standards and quality programming, it is important that students are familiar with swear words and their common substitutes, such as *f**k* (when written) or *the F-word*. It is also useful to know how to report how somebody swore at you: *He told me to F off.* You might like to ask if strong swear words are common in films, television and papers in the students' own culture(s) and how people feel about this. Remind students that using language like this can cause offence, and if they use it with people they don't know, they do risk offending them.

6 Collocations

Students could first attempt this without going back to the text. Remind students again of the importance of recording multi-word vocabulary like this in their notebooks.

Answers

strong public reaction
local television station
follow the plot
classic example
current climate of violence

Workbook

17 *-ed* adjectives, page 56

7 Talking Point

Give students time to do this ranking exercise on their own before discussing it in pairs. Another approach is to let students mingle after first doing it on their own as they try to find the student with the views closest to their own. You might want to teach some expressions which show strong disagreement (as long as students realise that these expressions are strong!):

That's ridiculous!
That's rubbish.
What a load of rubbish!
That's just not true.

And of course, some expressions for agreeing:

That's true, actually.
I agree with that.

Students could choose one of these opinions to write about for homework.

8 Enough

As a lead-in, put students in pairs and see if they can work out the reason why *enough* appears in different positions in the following:

It's not violent enough.	adjective + *enough*
There's not enough violence.	*enough* + noun
It's not big enough.	adjective + *enough*
There's not enough room.	*enough* + noun

After students have finished the simple matching exercise, get them to identify the phrases with *enough*.

Answers

1b 2a 3d 4c

Students should underline:

1. There isn't enough
2. isn't big enough
3. don't have enough time
4. not rich enough

9 Past perfect (G33)

The past perfect is conceptually not too difficult. However, if students find it difficult after reading the introduction to the exercise and the Grammar Commentary, you might like to illustrate the tense with a time-line on the board.

As the answers are somewhat open, you may need to walk around the class checking answers as students are writing. When they have finished writing, select a number of students to read out their answers. Check they are using the contracted form *I'd*, not *I had*.

Possible answers

2. I'd never made a speech in my life before.
3. I'd never met them before.
4. I'd never had/tried it before.
5. He'd been married once before.
6. They'd died in an earthquake.
7. We'd just had an argument.
8. I'd never actually flown before.

In the personalisation task, some of the sentences will obviously not apply to the students, but ask them to invent a way to complete them or tell them to ignore them and think of two or three different ones themselves. Put students in pairs to have brief conversations about their statements. Select a student first to give an example:

Jean:	*I'd never had prawns until I went to a Chinese restaurant.*
Teacher:	*And did you like them?*
Jean:	*No, not really.*
Teacher:	*Why not?*
Jean:	*Well, I've never really liked seafood and this was no exception.*

Workbook

20 Past perfect (joke), page 57

10 Film expressions

These expressions are extremely common when talking about your favourite films. After students have finished the matching exercise in pairs and you have checked it, they should cover the ends of the expressions in green, and in pairs take turns trying to recall the expressions using the beginnings in black as prompts. You could check this afterwards by calling out the first half of one of the expressions and then selecting a student to finish it. Do this a number of times and then get students to use the expressions to talk about one of their favourite films. This works best if you provide an example first.

Answers

1d 2f 3c 4a 5h 6g 7e 8b

Workbook

21 Writing, page 57

11 I've heard it's really good

These conversations are about films that the speakers haven't seen, but are thinking about going to see. Although the conversations are about films, much of the highlighted language could be used to talk about other things that people are thinking of seeing or reading or even buying. Point this out to students.

Answers

Conversation 1: b a c d
Conversation 2: a c b d
Conversation 3: d b a e c

Students should practise the conversations in pairs before attempting to use the highlighted expressions to talk about a film they'd like to see. One approach to this is to put students in threes, with the third person listening for the highlighted expressions and awarding a point for each expression heard. The winner then becomes the listener/scorer and so on.

12 Television vocabulary

Students could do this exercise on their own using a dictionary where necessary. After they have checked answers in pairs they can discuss the follow-up questions. These can then be discussed as a whole class. You may need to explain that:

BBC = the British Broadcasting Corporation
ITV = Independent Television

Answers

remote, channel, advertisements, aerials, digital, cable, documentaries, series

13 Asking questions

These are typical questions that are asked about films or television programmes and should be learned as whole expressions. Remind students they may want to add some of this language to the Expression Organiser on page 190. At this stage just get students to complete the exercise, as the pronunciation and practice will come later.

Answers

1f 2a 3g 4c 5b 6e 7h 8d

After students have read the examples in the Real English note, see if they can come up with an example sentence of their own. You could also point out that *some* used in this way often suggests that you don't think it's worth mentioning the name of the person. For example:

Who was that on the phone?
> Some guy from work. He's locked himself in again and wants the keys.

What's this programme?
> Some old professor talking about world conflicts. It's not worth watching.

And when you can't answer! (T50)

Use the tape as a model to let students practise saying the phrases several times until they can say them naturally.

Answers

1. Sorry, my mind's gone completely blank.
2. Wait, it'll come to me in a minute.
3. Wait, it's on the tip of my tongue.
4. Sorry, I can't remember off the top of my head.

I need to look it up = number 4
I can almost, but not quite, remember = numbers 2 and 3
I've forgotten = number 1

14 Pronunciation (T51)

This provides pronunciation practice and practice of the questions and expressions introduced in exercise 13. Notice that there is also a chance to practise these questions and the *I can't remember* expressions in a personalisation task.

15 Contradicting (T52)

It is harder to disagree or contradict in another language than it is to agree. Not only must you use the right expression, you must also say it in the correct way. Use the tape to model the all-important stress and intonation needed here.

Answers

1d 2c 3f 4e 5a 6b

Round up the exercise by getting students to contradict you. Say things like:

Carlo, you don't like sport, do you? (if you know he does like sport.)
Maria, you're not coming to school next week, are you?

Then put students in pairs to do the same thing.

16 Film knowledge

You could begin by asking students to identify the people in the photos and explain why they are famous (*Marilyn Monroe, Marlon Brando and Alfred Hitchcock.*)

The exercise can then be done in pairs, or with an older class who might know more about many of the people in the list, it is better as a game. Divide the class into two teams. The teams take turns to give one fact about the names listed. A team gets one point for each fact. If they are unable to offer a fact about a name, this passes over to the other team who have the chance to earn an extra point.

Vocabulary

Adjective collocations

1. filthy dirty 2. boiling hot 3. soaking wet
4. freezing cold 5. crystal clear 6. dead tired

Idioms

1. razor sharp 2. brand new 3. stark naked 4. wide
awake 5. dirt cheap 6. fast asleep 7. dead easy
8. rock hard

Synonyms

1g 2e 3h 4a 5f 6c 7d 8b
a. terrible/horrendous car crash
b. clever/brilliant composer
c. annoying/irritating habit
d. weird/strange coincidence

Adjectives

Very good	Mildly critical	Very bad
terrific	a bit bland	dreadful
excellent	very ordinary	horrible
wonderful	nothing special	horrendous
marvellous	on the dull side	dire
brilliant	not very inspiring	terrible
superb	a bit disappointing	awful

Audiences

1. audience 2. congregation 3. fans 4. viewers
5. spectators 6. on-lookers

Extra workbook exercises

13 Pop bands, page 55
15 Prepositional phrases, page 55
16 Typical mistakes (prepositions), page 55
18 Expressions with *out of*, page 56
19 Collocations, page 57

Review: Units 7 and 8

1 Tenses

1. I went 2. I've played 3. Have you been staying in
4. I've asked him 5. That must've been 6. I've been
trying 7. Did you speak 8. that must be 9. I haven't
seen

2 Multiple choice

1b 2a 3a 4a 5b 6b 7b 8a

3 Expressions

1. It's on the tip of my tongue. 2. Not a lot, really.
3. He's not exactly ... 4. They weren't as good as I'd
expected 5. That reminds me. 6. I haven't seen you
for ages.

4 Conversation

1a 2d 3f 4e 5c 6b

Collocations

1e 2h 3d 4g 5f 6c 7a 8b

Idioms

1d 2h 3g 4a 5b 6e 7f 8c

For and *since*

1. for 2. since 3. since 4. for 5. since 6. for 7. since
8. for

Real English

1e 2a 3d 4b 5g 6c 7f

Vocabulary quiz

1. No. It means you can't see the purpose of it.
2. Motives. 3. It makes you cry. 4. No. 5. Yes. 6. In
the future. 7. In the sky and in films (or on TV).
8. Sheep, onions, vegetables, even grandmothers!
9. No, they decide if the film is suitable for different
age groups etc. 10. No. 11. You are recommending it.
12. Over the top. 13. 100 years ago or more. 14. No –
you've known him/her for a long time. 15. No, it
means you don't like it. 16. A *plot* is used specifically
when talking about the events in a book, a play or a
film so it is a more specific use than the more general
word *story*. 17. In your life. 18. No, you are giving
permission. 19. Almost certainly not. 20. Emotionally.

Unit 9a
Cars and cities

Unit overview

Topic

Traffic problems in cities; the general issue of change.

The dialogue

Chris and Claire give their views on a local traffic problem.

Input language

* Suggestions with *if* – *It'd be a good idea if they ... . It'd be far better if they ... .*
* Collocations – *a difficult question, strong views, cause problems* etc
* Disagreeing – *I agree up to a point but ... .*
* Impersonal *they* – *They should do something about it.*
* The passive – *The streets are never cleaned round here.*
* Comparatives – *much safer, far slower* etc
* Animal idioms – *I do all the donkey work.*

Reading text

Global warming – Is it worth worrying about?

The language strip

Ask students to read the first sentence: *Oh no, look at the traffic.* Ask when someone would say or think this. When was the last time students said or thought this? Then get them to look at the last sentence in the strip: *If only more people used public ... .* Ask students what they think comes next (transport).

Ask students to find two sentences with the word *policeman.* With a partner, discuss the difference. There is a Real English note on *sleeping policemen* at the bottom of the page.

Ask students to find three expressions with *just.* What are the equivalent expressions in their own language?

1 Traffic survey

Before looking at the list, ask the students what sort of traffic problems they have in their own towns or cities. Then put them into small groups and ask them to list as many solutions to traffic problems as they can think of. Then get them to compare their lists with the list in the book. Check students understand the words and expressions and, in particular, point out the collocations in this list:

> *install speed cameras, accident black spots, quiet streets, on-street parking (as opposed to parking in car parks), pedestrianise the main shopping area, provide better public transport, ban all cars from the town centre, double the number of, a one-way system.*

Encourage students to record these collocations in this form in their notebooks. Remind them how important it is not to break expressions down into individual words.

Put students in pairs to do the ranking activity. You might want to provide some sentence starters to help students talk about the list:

> *The best way to deal with traffic problems would be to ...*
> *That wouldn't really work because ...*
> *That would be a waste of time because ...*
> *I think it might / would be better to ...*

Collect the four solutions with the highest priority from each group and write them on the board to work out as a class which approach to improving traffic problems is the most popular.

Photo opportunity

Either before or after the ranking activity, use the photograph to explain and talk about *traffic wardens.* Do students like traffic wardens? In the UK they just put parking tickets on illegally parked cars. Ask what the equivalent job is in the students' country and what exactly they do. Have any of the students had a parking ticket? How much did they have to pay?

Use the other photo on this page to discuss cycle lanes; are they useful? Are they dangerous?

You might also point out that the street on page 136 is a *one-way street.*

2 While you listen (T53)

Read the introduction to the listening and then exploit the conversation in the usual way.

Answers

1. The speed of cars; a pedestrian crossing in the wrong place; too many cars parked near the crossing.
2. Move the crossing and put sleeping policemen or speed cameras on the road to slow the traffic down.

After completing the gap-fill stage, draw students' attention to the Real English vocabulary items.

Workbook

2 Auxiliary verbs, page 58
4 The fact that, page 59

3 Your view

This is probably best done as pair work, then discussed openly as a class by selecting students to give their answers. You could take a vote on the worst city for driving.

Workbook

6 Traffic offences, page 59

4 Suggestions with *if* (G34)

We often make suggestions for improving things with *if*.

You might need to teach *absolute chaos* and *multi-storey (car park)*. Walk round the class and check that students are writing the '*if*-sentence starters' correctly in the summary section. Each of the four '*if*-sentence starters' appears twice in the eight sentences.

Answers

1d 2b 3a 4c 5g 6h 7f 8e

Each of these sentence starters needs to be learned as a single item of vocabulary. So, when students have identified and written them in the summary, model them, paying particular attention to the contractions. Practise saying them, chorally and individually, until students can say them fluently. Write them on the board and gradually erase more and more words, seeing if students can still remember the expressions.

The sentence starters are:

a. It'd be more useful if ...
b. What would be really great is if ...
c. I think it'd be a really good idea if ...
d. It'd be (far) better if . . .

Finally, let students read the Grammar Commentary on page 185.

Workbook

1 'If' suggestions, page 58

5 Collocations

This exercise implicitly introduces more expressions for talking about your views on things, focusing on the common collocations (adjective–noun and verb–noun) that appear in these expressions. If you have time, you might see if the students can use their dictionaries to find two more verb and/or adjective collocations for each noun. Good mono-lingual dictionaries usually contain such collocations in the example sentences for the headword.

Answers

1. a difficult question 2. strong views 3. tackle that problem 4. raises the question of 5. cause problems 6. major issue 7. different views 8. avoid the issue

Students should record these collocations (*a difficult question, strong views* etc) at the very least. It would be better, however, if they recorded the whole sentences, even if they know all the other words. This is because the surrounding co-text is related to the collocations and their use. Remind students that the more context they record, the easier it will be for them to recall and use the language again.

6 Personal opinions

Before students do the pair work, you should model the expressions and let students practise saying them after you. Students should underline the main stressed syllable in the words in green in the box. You also might need to explain *kilt*, as worn by Scottish men.

Teach the expression *It's a good idea in theory, but in practice ...* and give an example:

> *One car per family is a good idea in theory, but in practice it'll never work because ...*

7 Role Play

Before you do this exercise, give students time to look at the language in exercises 4, 5 and 6 again, and perhaps also look through their own notebooks. You could also create a gap-fill exercise by writing the expressions you want the students to revise on the board, but leaving out the occasional word and then asking students to complete the whole expression. For example:

> *What . . . . . . be really . . . . . . is if . . . .*
> *That's a . . . . . . question to . . . .*

Choose the gap so that it is easy to put back what is missing; this is an activity to jog the memory, not to test students.

Before you begin the role play, pre-teach *colleague, old-fashioned* and *network system*.

Then divide the class into groups of three if possible. Set the scene by telling them that they are having a drink after work and start discussing the things that they are not happy about. One person must begin by saying: *You know, I just can't believe that we're still using those computers ...* (write this on the board). The others join in and they all make suggestions on improving the situation before one of them raises the next problem on the list and so on.

Encourage students to use the expressions during the role plays by walking around the class and feeding in appropriate expressions where students are having difficulty. Give feedback on how the groups performed and then ask them to do it again, putting your feedback into practice.

The final question could be discussed as a whole class activity. Give students two minutes to think about the question and then let individuals who have something to say tell the class.

Workbook

12 Complaining, page 62

8 Disagreeing (T54)

Before students do the second stage of the exercise when they agree rather than disagree, point out the difference in meaning and intonation between *Yes, I know what you mean but ...* (disagreeing) and *Oh yes, I know what you mean* (agreeing). Suggest that students could use the expressions in exercise 6 to follow up this agreeing expression when doing the exercises for the second time.

Answers

a. Well, I agree up to a point but ...
b. Yes, I know what you mean but ...
c. Yes, but don't you think that ...
d. Yes, but don't forget that ...

Workbook

15 Agreeing expressions, page 62
You could look at this with the class before students do the second stage of the activity above.

9 Impersonal *they* (G35)

This is a common use of *they* for referring to the groups of nameless people from the council, government or organisations who provide services, collect taxes, erect buildings etc and who generally have an effect on our daily lives. The Grammar Commentary on page 185 highlights a slightly different use of *they* – for when we are unsure or don't want to reveal the sex of someone who is being talked about and as a result we cannot use the usual male or female pronouns. Students will need time to reflect on the discussion questions before talking about their answers with a partner.

Answers

1. the police
2. the people who collect the rubbish!
3. the government
4. the check-in desk staff

Global Warming

First, check students know what *global warming* and *climate* mean. Then an interesting way to approach a factual text like this is to get students to put a tick after each item of information in the text that they already knew, a cross after each piece of information that they didn't and a question mark after anything they disagree with or are unsure about. They could then compare with a partner before doing the Talking Point. Alternatively, use questions 1-3 in the Talking Point to lead into the reading text.

10 Talking Point

Begin with either question 2 as a general comprehension question, or question 1, asking students if they are personally worried about the effects of global warming.

You might also need to provide a few model sentences of *prepared to* to make the meaning of the expression clear in this context (it is very similar in meaning to *willing to*.) For example:

*I'm prepared to stop smoking if we have children.
I'm only prepared to let you join the course if you promise to work hard.*

Answer

In the past twenty years the earth's temperature has been increasing by 0.1° every ten years; the polar ice caps are melting; the sea level is rising; areas of the world will get wetter or drier and diseases like malaria will spread to places where they are currently unknown.

11 The passive (G36)

As a lead-in, write the two examples on the board and see if students can suggest what is different about the two sentences and, more importantly, **when** (and why) they might choose to use each one. Also ask what could replace the subject pronoun *they* (*The local council* have knocked down the cinema.) and how natural these suggestions sound. (See exercise 9 above.) Then get them to read the Grammar Commentary on page 185 to see if they were correct.

Answers

1. An old bomb's been found in the town centre.
2. The High Street's been closed.
3. The swimming pool's being cleaned today.
4. A multi-storey car park's being built.
5. The rubbish is collected on Wednesdays.
6. The streets are never cleaned round here.

7. That restaurant was closed down last year.
8. Rats were found in the kitchen.
9. The toilets were still being cleaned when the Queen arrived.
10. The road was being repaired all last week.
11. A new airport's going to be built.
12. The street lighting's going to be improved.
13. Something should be done about the litter.
14. More rubbish bins should be provided.

Workbook

9 The passive, page 60
There is a 'passive joke' on page 60 which you may want to read to the class. Read it a second time and ask students to identify the two examples of the passive.

12 Talking Point

Ask if the students have ever heard of the famous English town of Brighton and if they can tell you anything about it.

Brighton is a popular seaside town on the south coast about 50 miles south of London. It has a lot of visitors so it has a lot of restaurants, bars and clubs. The club scene is one of the liveliest outside London. Many people have heard of Brighton because of Graham Greene's novel, Brighton Rock.

Lots of buildings have recently been modernised or have changed their use. In particular, several banks have now become restaurants or bars.

Ask if the students' own cities have undergone any major changes recently such as more cafés, more pedestrian areas or more trendy bars (check *trendy* at this point).

Then point out the two example sentences:

It used to be a ...
It's been turned into a ...

Do the first one together in class, then put students in pairs for 2-4.

Answers

1. It used to be an estate agent's. It's been turned into a restaurant.
2. It used to be an insurance office. It's been turned into a trendy bar.
3. It used to be a bank. It's been turned into a fish and chip restaurant.
4. It used to be a public toilet. It's been turned into a sandwich bar.

You may need to introduce the following variation of the above expressions to help students do the final discussion exercise in pairs:

There's a building in my home town which used to be a ... , but it's been turned into a ... .

Encourage students to give their opinions on the changes.

13 Pronunciation (T55)

Play the tape for students to listen and repeat. Ask students to create one or two statements with this pattern. For example: *Brazil are a far better football team than England.*

14 Comparatives

This follows on from the previous exercise. As some of the comparatives in colour might fit into a number of the sentences, students need to examine the co-text carefully.

Answers

1. much faster 2. far cheaper 3. much more expensive 4. much more difficult 5. far easier
6. far slower 7. far more dangerous 8. much safer

Afterwards, you could ask students in pairs to think of other things that are *much safer, much faster, far more dangerous than they used to be.* Make a list of these on the board. This could become a short written homework task. Ask students to write about their ideas in about 100 words or so.

15 Animal idioms

The most common forms of these animal idioms are:

It's gone to the dogs.
I think I smell a rat.
I (just) do all the donkey work.
He's got ants in his pants.
Don't let the cat out of the bag.
You can do that till the cows come home (but it won't help.)
I'm the black sheep of the family.
You sent us on a wild goose chase.

Once the students have completed the exercise, you could write these on the board for the students to record in their notebooks as models. Then rub them off and using just the animal name as the cue, see if students can recall the whole expressions. Then, in pairs, ask them to think of other contexts where the idioms might be used appropriately.

16 A really major issue

Before students do this exercise, go back and revise some of the expressions in this unit so far (See the notes for exercise 7 for a way of doing this.) They should also do the translation exercises on page 191. You could ask students to write about one of their chosen problems for homework, encouraging them to use some of the language they have learned in this unit.

Unit 9b
Annoying things

Unit overview

Topic

Anything which annoys you.

Text

A town council decides to do something about the mess caused by chewing gum.

Input language

- Phrasal verbs – *put up with it, go on about it* etc
- Complaining – *I wish they wouldn't, That's the last thing I need.*
- Fixed expressions – *It's not the end of the world. Don't let it get you down.*
- Was/were going to – *I thought it was going to be a five-star hotel but ...*

The language strip

Ask students to find expressions which you can say to someone who is annoyed.

Get them to find expressions beginning with 'I'. Have they used, or would they say these in English? What is the equivalent in their own language?

Do the same with expressions beginning with 'It'.

Ask students to look at the photo on page 143. Then, with a partner, ask them to read the language strip and find any sentences which they could use to talk about what they see.

1 It really drives me mad

Continuing with the photo, ask students if this sort of thing can be seen in their own towns or cities, why it happens and if it annoys them or not. You could also ask them what the dirtiest city they have ever been to is and what is the cleanest. Would they prefer to live in a dirty, but lively city, or a clean, but culturally dead, city?

See if students can work out the meaning of the idiom, *It really drives me mad.* Can they think of any other similar expressions? *(It drives me up the wall.)* Then read through 1-7 with the students, helping them with the meaning of any unfamiliar vocabulary before they do the exercise in pairs. Find out what the class thinks are the most annoying things from the list and follow up the pair work with a whole-class discussion about how to prevent these things from happening. Refer students to the *if*-sentence starters for providing suggestions on page 138.

Ask students if there are any other annoying things that they *have to live with*. (If necessary, teach this expression.)

2 While reading

Before you get students to look at the introductory questions, ask them to look up the word *sticky* in their dictionaries. Check they understand the collocations *sticky situation* and *sticky problem*. Then look at the photograph together and ask if the scene looks familiar. Relate the title of the text to the picture and ask a student to explain the pun in the title. Ask students to guess what the article is about before they read it and answer the three questions.

Answers

1. The pavements are covered in chewing gum which costs £6000 a year to clear up.
2. Complaints from shopkeepers, locals and visitors about the mess.
3. Boards will be put up for people to stick their chewing gum on when they have finished with it.

3 Word check

Answers

1. put 2. mess 3. act 4. facelift 5. flooded

Highlight the common collocations or expressions that appear with these words:

Put it up on the board.
It's in such a mess.
If they don't act soon, then …
It badly needs a facelift.
flooded with applications

4 Comprehension check

Get students to do this in pairs, then check it with the whole class, following up with a short class discussion around the questions printed in bold.

Answers

1. £6000 a year 2. a facelift to the town centre 3. £100
4. the centre of a round target like the one used in darts

5 Phrasal verbs

First get students to complete the matching exercise in the blue box to check their initial understanding of the phrasal verbs. Select students to read out the matched sentences, checking pronunciation. In b, *state* means *condition* in *Just look at the state of it*. A similar expression is *Look at the state we're / you're in*.

Answers

1d 2e 3c 4b 5a

The exercise below the blue box provides students with two extra contexts for each of these verbs.

Answers

1. end up, end up 2. put up with, put up with
3. get away with, get away with 4. mess up, mess up
5. going on about, going on about

This exercise also allows students to see the patterns associated with these verbs. They have to identify these patterns for the first question after the exercise. They are:

1. end up + *-ing*
2. put up with + object + *-ing*
3. get away with + noun
4. mess up + noun
5. going on about how + clause

Point out the expression:

If (something doesn't change / improve), I'm going to end up going mad.

Ask students to complete the sentence in a way which is true for them.

Point out the expression: *They let her get away with murder* in number 3. See if students can remember any of the 'death-related' expressions from page 94.

Workbook

11 Phrasal verbs, page 61

6 Complaining (T56)

You might want to use the jokes on page 63 of the Workbook to introduce this activity.

See if students can fill the gaps in the conversations before hearing the tape. Alternatively, introduce the first situation (complaining about a meal) and play the tape of the conversation twice with students listening only. They then read and fill in the gaps. Do the same with the second conversation.

Answers

Oh, it was awful! The food wasn't very good. **It would've been OK if that was the only problem, but** the waiters were really rude as well. **And then, to top the whole thing off**, they tried to overcharge us. Then when we complained about it, they **made it sound as if** it was our fault.
Not very well actually. **I've got a bit of a problem with** my timetable this term. **I mean, the last thing I need** is three lectures on a Friday. **I wish they wouldn't** change the timetable every term. Last term was much better.

Get students to practise the conversations in pairs. Walk around the class, checking that students sound annoyed, and modelling pronunciation where necessary.

If students have difficulty with the expression: *It's the last thing I need*, give another example to make the meaning clear:

> *I've been working hard all day and I'm exhausted. The last thing I need is to come home and find that all our relations are here.*

A similar expression to *And to top the whole thing off ...* is *And to make matters worse ... .*

Workbook

Use 12 Complaining, on page 62 if you have not already done so.

7 Role play

Before you do the role play, give students plenty of time to look back at the language they need and think about what they want to say. You might want them to write their complaints to begin with and to do the task two or three times, using their notes less each time. Provide the following example to give students an idea of what you want:

> *I went round to Liz's place last night. She made it sound as if it was really close to the town centre, but I got totally lost. First of all, I took the wrong turning off the motorway, then I went up a one-way street the wrong way. The map was useless.*

A fun way to extend this activity is to have a complaining knock-out competition. Ask for two volunteers. They each have a turn to complain in front of the class using one of the situations in the blue box. The class decides who is the best complainer and then the winner has another turn to complain about another situation, competing against the next volunteer and so on. The losers are removed from the competition. This continues until all volunteers have had a turn complaining and have been knocked out except the one remaining student, who is the best complainer.

8 Useful fixed expressions (T57)

This exercise takes this language area a step further and introduces a number of expressions that are typical responses when people are complaining to us. Do the first one together. Ask students for another word for *bug* in mini-conversation 1, then refer them to the Real English at the bottom of the page. Let students check their answers using the tape. Then practise the conversations in pairs.

Answers

1. things like that don't really bother me.
2. It's not the end of the world.
3. Don't let it get you down.
4. there's nothing you can do about it.

9 Talking Point

This exercise provides practice of the expressions in exercise 8. Model and practise the expressions before students do the mingling activity. Remind students or elicit from them what they can say if they want to agree. For example:

> *Oh, I know what you mean.*
> *It's a pain in the neck, isn't it?*
> *It bugs me, too.*

10 Was / were going to (G37)

This grammar exercise presents a grammatical structure as part of an expression and also places it within a useful and memorable context – namely, complaining about a holiday from hell! Ask students to read the examples in the blue box before you ask them to study the Grammar Commentary on page 186 together.

Answers

1. I thought we were going to stay ...
2. It said there was going to be a drinks party ...
3. It said the new swimming pool was going to be ready ...
4. I thought the hotel was going to be a five-minute walk ...
5. They said every room was going to have fresh flowers ...
6. The brochure said that we were going to have new towels ...
7. I thought we were going to be met ...
8. I thought our towels were going to be changed every day ...
9. It said we were going to be taken on a moonlight cruise ...

Workbook

16 Was / were going to, page 63

11 Your complaints

This exercise personalises and consolidates the structure introduced in exercise 10. Students work alone with the ideas in the blue box and then compare what they have written with a partner. Ask a few students to read their statements to the class.

Possible answers

I thought it was going to be a little bit curly, but this is ridiculous.
I thought I was going to lose weight easily, but it's really slow.
I thought it was going to be reliable, but I've had so many problems with it.
I thought it was going to be a comedy, but it was more like a thriller.
I thought it was going to be on at ten o'clock, but they changed it to eleven.

Then ask students if they have any other real-life experiences they can share. They will probably need to add time expressions:

Last Monday I thought I was going to be late for my English class, but I wasn't.
When I was younger, I always thought I was going to be rich and famous, but now I'm just a teacher.

12 One final complaint

First, either as a class, or in groups of two or three, students say whether they would complain in these situations or not. Write the following expressions on the board and encourage students to use them during the discussion:

I probably wouldn't say anything.
I'd complain immediately.
I'd just put up with it, I think.
I'm not sure what I would do.

Next, ask students in pairs to choose four of the situations and write what they would say if they did complain. Help students, supplying the expressions they need to complain appropriately, and conduct a general class feedback on expressions to use in these situations.

You could use some of these situations for short role plays to finish the lesson, or at the start of the next one, to recycle language from the unit.

Workbook

13 Complaining / apologising, page 62 will help students prepare for a role play for the hotel situation.

Remind students to translate the expressions in the Expressions Organiser on page 191.

Workbook

18 Writing, page 63

Vocabulary page

Answers

Fixed expressions

1d 2a 3b 4c

Expressions with *bother*

1f 2g 3a 4h 5d 6e 7b 8c

Driving vocabulary

taken a wrong turning
the wrong direction
did a U-turn
a one-way street
headlights coming towards me
slammed on my brakes
tried to pull over
run out of petrol

1. take a wrong turn 2. go in the wrong direction
3. do a U-turn 4. go down a one-way street 5. slam
on the brakes 6. run out of petrol

Cities

1. capital 2. industrial 3. cosmopolitan 4. inner city
5. historic 6. shanty towns 7. centre 8. overcrowded

Extra workbook exercises

3   Cars, page 58
5   Traffic signs, page 59
7   Compound adjectives, page 59
8   *Make* and *let*, page 60
10 Expressions with *all*, page 61
14 *Explain* and *ask*, page 62

Unit 10a
Your future

Unit overview

Topic

Plans, hopes and aspirations.

The dialogue

Rachel and Nick talk about their plans after leaving college.

Language input

- Starting with *what* – *What I'd really like to do is ...* etc
- Expressions – *I'm happy doing what I'm doing. I can't really say yet* etc
- Planning structures – *I might try and find ... I can see myself ...* etc
- Sentence adverbs – *Hopefully, Realistically* etc
- If-expressions – *if all goes well* etc
- The present perfect – *As soon as I've finished this course ...* etc

Reading text

Chat rooms – a good idea or a sad hobby?

The language strip

Get students to find expressions beginning with 'I'. Have they or would they say these in English? What is the equivalent in their own language?

Write on the board: *What do you think you'll be doing in five years' time?* Ask students to find any sentences that could answer this question. Then ask a few students the same question. Explain that this unit will help them to talk about their future hopes and plans.

1 Optimistic about the future? (T58)

Ask students: *Are you generally an optimist or a pessimist?* Spend a minute listening to their answers then tell them they are going to listen to eight statements on the tape. They must decide whether they agree with the statements or not. Play the statements from the tape, stopping after each one and giving the students a few moments to write down whether they agree or disagree. Do this as a listening-only exercise with their books closed. Then ask them to compare their answers with a partner and justify their choices.

If students need to hear the statements again, play the tape but this time with students following in their books.

With the same partner, they should complete the sentence in green with *a pessimist* and *an optimist* and follow this up by deciding if the statements were optimistic or pessimistic.

They can also decide if the partner they are working with is a pessimist or an optimist.

Answers

An optimist is someone who always thinks the glass is half full, while a pessimist always thinks it's half empty.

1, 3, 6, 8 = optimistic
2, 4, 5, 7 = pessimistic

2 Talking Point

After students have finished discussing these questions with a partner or in small groups, select a few students to give their thoughts and develop this into a class discussion.

Photo opportunity

The people in the photo gave up their jobs to live in trees for many months because they felt so strongly about trees being cut down.

Find out if anyone has been involved in any protest action groups. Ask students to name some protest groups or organisations (Greenpeace, Animal Liberation Front, Amnesty International). Ask if students think these types of groups really make the world a better place. Does anyone belong to, or give money to, a particular group?

3 While you listen (T59)

Read the introduction together and explain the meaning of the expression: *What do you see yourself doing in the future?* Then get students to read through the statements about Rachel and Nick in 1 – 4 before you play the tape. Play the tape once all the way through and ask students just to listen. Ask them to discuss 1 – 4 with a partner. Play the tape again, pausing so that students have time to fill in the gaps with their partner.

Answers

1. Nick's thinking about doing an art course but it depends on his results.
2. He'd like to do a French course in Paris but he probably won't have enough money.
3. Rachel wants to learn to drive and buy a car.
4. If she can find a good job then she'll stay where she is. Otherwise, she'll probably go back to Glasgow.

Let students read the dialogue and see how many gaps they can fill in from memory. Play the tape again with pauses so that students can hear and write down exactly what was said.

See if anyone can explain the title, *Now you're talking!* which also comes at the end of the conversation.

Refer students to the Real English note. Ask a few students if their country has any friendly rivalry with another country. If so, is there an affectionate term they call each other?

4 Talking Point

As usual, this is best done as pair work first, leading to a whole-class discussion as you select a few students to share their answers. You'll need to teach the expression *on the spur of the moment*.

5 Pronunciation (T60)

It is very difficult to say what *really* means in this context. It seems to make speakers' statements sound less certain or less direct. Rather than trying to understand a definition of the word, however, students need to get a feel for how to use it.

The same is true of *then*, although the Real English note at the bottom of the page helps explain how to use the word.

In the examples given here, *actually* is used to contradict, or announce surprising information.

Let students listen to the first two sentences in green. Say these yourself a number of times for students to repeat after you. Then play the rest of the tape, dialogue by dialogue, with pauses for students to repeat the relevant expressions. Then let students practise the conversations in pairs. Finish with students writing one short two-line dialogue for each of the words and practising them with a partner.

6 Starting with *what*

Say the examples in the blue box for the students to repeat after you. Point out the difference between:

really need to = necessity
would really like to = what you want to do
I was thinking of doing = something you're considering

Answers

1. What I really need to do is learn/start learning Japanese.
2. What I'd really like to do is to buy a flat in the next couple of years.
3. What I really need to do is start saving.
4. What I was thinking of doing is travelling around India.

5. What I'd really like to do is start a family as soon as I get married.
6. What I was thinking of doing is going abroad for Christmas this year.

When students have finished, go back to the prompts in the exercise to point out some collocations and expressions that students should record in their notebooks:

in the next couple of years, desperately need to, in the not-too-distant future, as soon as (you) get married, go abroad

Add other related collocations such as *in the distant future, in the near future*. The workbook has more examples like this (page 67).

Grammar in context

As students are completing these on their own, walk around the class and check they are forming the expressions and what follows correctly. Help where necessary.

Workbook

1 Starting with *what*, page 64

7 Plans for the future

Once students have completed the sentences and checked with a partner, model the pronunciation of the expressions and get students to repeat them after you. To help students remember the expressions, write the words in colour on the board and, with their books closed, select students to try and recall the whole expressions. Get students to translate the **whole** expressions into their own language. The mini-conversations provide contexts for the expressions. Once students have completed the gaps, they should practise these in pairs.

Answers

a. perfectly happy b. change c. see myself
d. wait and see e. take things f. can't really

1. I just take things as they come
2. My plans change fairly often
3. I can't see myself staying there for much longer.
4. I'm perfectly happy doing what I'm doing.
5. I'll just have to wait and see what happens.
6. I can't really say yet. It all depends on my girlfriend.

8 Planning structures

These sentence starters are typical responses to questions about future plans. Unlike the more vague responses in exercise 7, these discuss more specific plans. Make sure you draw these collocations to students' attention:

find a new job, going back to university, spend a bit more time with my girlfriend

Answers

1 c,g 2 b,e 3 d,f 4 a,h 5 m,o 6 l,n 7 i,q 8 k,p 9 j,r

A fun way for students to practise these 'planning structures' is with a card game.

1. You need 36 small cards. On 18 cards write one of the expressions from a-r.

2. Make two sets of 9 with a 'planning structure' on each card.

3. Spread the cards out, face down on a table. The students sit around the table and take turns selecting any two cards and seeing if they match to make a complete 'planning structure' as in exercise 8.

If they don't, they put the cards back in the same place and the turn passes to the next person. If they do match, the student says the complete expression, keeps the cards, and has another go.

The winner is the person who collects most cards.

Workbook

2 I might try and ... , page 64
3 Planning structures, page 65
9 Future collocations, page 66

9 A year away

One approach to this discussion exercise is to get students to put 1-6 in order, from most to least appealing. They could then justify their choices with a partner or in small groups. You could put some useful expressions on the board:

I'd love to ...
I'd quite like to ...
I could imagine working / going / sailing ... etc
I could see myself working / going sailing ... etc
That's not my cup of tea, really.
That's not my sort of thing, really.

10 Sentence adverbs

These particular sentence adverbs occur frequently in conversations about future plans. Practise the pronunciation of the words before students do the first exercise, which provides a clear definition for each of the adverbs.

Answers

a. Eventually b. Ideally c. Hopefully d. Realistically
e. Basically

In the personalisation task, give your own example for number 1 before students complete the sentences. Then, discuss what verb patterns immediately follow the sentence starters. They are all followed by a verb + the infinitive form except:

I can see myself + -ing
I really like + -ing
I'd like to end up + -ing

While students are completing the sentences in the personalisation exercise, walk around the class checking and helping students with any difficulties.

Workbook

6 Sentence adverbs, page 66

11 Finding out more

Once you have modelled the questions yourself, select two students to read out each mini-conversation. Do this a number of times. Students then work with the same partner as in exercise 10 and try to recall two of the things their partner was thinking of doing in the future. They use these to find out more about their partner's plans using the expressions in red. Encourage students to keep the conversations going for as long as possible. Recycle some expressions from exercise 7 to help these conversations develop:

I'll just have to wait and see what happens.
I can't really say yet. It all depends.
My plans change fairly often.

Round up by asking students who know about the plans of other students in the room to go and ask them how these plans are coming on.

12 Chat rooms

Get a few students to explain what a *chat room* is. Ask students to read the text and answer the questions in pairs. Remember that these texts are to stimulate discussion rather than as detailed reading comprehension, so do not get too side-tracked by a lot of vocabulary questions.

The questions, asking students to describe a chat room to someone who doesn't own a computer and someone who lived 100 years ago, are supposed to be fun, but you could ask students to look again at the Real English note on page 99 and recycle some of that vague language here.

Some helpful definitions for technophobes:

A 'chat room' is a page (or site) on the internet where you can send and receive messages from other internet users in real time – it's a bit like using a telephone, except you are connected to more than one person and you are using a keyboard rather than a phone.

A 'server' is the organisation which you connect to through a telephone line via a modem that supplies you with your internet access.

A 'search engine' is an internet program used to find information providers on the web.

13 Talking Point

With technophobic classes, the Talking Point answers are likely to be all negative and won't make for a very productive pair work discussion. If this is the case, then do this as a class discussion exercise and get those who have used a chat room to discuss their experiences using the questions as a guide. As a follow-up, if possible, you should encourage those students who haven't used a chat room before to access one at your school, an internet café, a friend's place or at home. Set this up as a project to be completed before the end of their course and when they've done it, get students to talk about their experiences. Not only are chat rooms a good place for students to practise their English, but in the process they will also acquire a lot of useful internet language.

14 Collocations

This exercise consolidates collocations related to the internet. Students could store these in an 'internet' page in their notebooks.

Answers

1. access 2. enter, visit 3. search 4. part 5. chosen
6. click 7. details 8. real

15 If-expressions

Choosing the correct tense form is only a small part of talking about the future. Students also need a number of expressions which express attitude, certainty or uncertainty, and contingency, for example. These expressions enable students to do this.

Answers

1. goes 2. goes 3. falls 4. fails 5. goes 6. work

The if-expressions are:

1. If all goes well ...
2. If everything goes according to plan ...
3. If that falls through ...
4. If all else fails ...
5. If nothing goes wrong ...
6. If that doesn't work ...

After students have underlined the 'If- expressions' above, get them to sort them into those which are optimistic and those which are pessimistic (1 and 2 are optimistic; the others are pessimistic.)

Draw students' attention to the Real English note.

Workbook

4 Expressions with *if*, page 65
5 If + *things*, page 65

16 Talking Point

This exercise provides an opportunity for freer practice of the *if*-expressions from exercise 15. Numbers 4 and 5 could also be seen from the birds' point of view.

Answers

1. Well, if all goes well, I should be working for a top law firm within a few weeks.
2. If everything goes according to plan, I'll be in Delhi by the end of the year.
3. If everything goes according to plan, we're going to get married next June.
4. If nothing goes wrong, we/they should be in South Africa by Friday!
5. If all goes well, I'll be eating one of those next month. (The turkeys might be thinking: If all else fails, we'll all attack the farmer and escape through the gate!)

Get pairs to compare their sentences and select the best ones to be read out in front of the class.

17 The present perfect (G38)

Conjunctions

This exercise looks at the present perfect used with conjunctions that introduce future plans or intentions. Point out the pattern:

As soon as + present perfect + going to

Get students to read the Grammar Commentary on page 186 first and then do the exercise.

Answers

1. Once I've saved up enough money, ...
2. As soon as my brother's finished his military service, ...
3. The minute I've finished my exams, ...

Number three is the most emphatic. It sounds the most immediate.

Grammar in context 1

In this exercise different verb forms are used in the second clause (instead of *going to).*

Answers

1. Once you've finished 2. The minute you've got
3. Once I've been 4. as soon as you've discussed it
5. As soon as I've visited John 6. once you've opened
the packaging

As students are completing the sentence starters,
check that they are forming the structures correctly
and help where necessary. Get students to take turns
using their sentences to begin short conversations
modelled on the example at the bottom of page 156.

Grammar in context 2

Students use the conjunctions + the present perfect to
make true sentences using the prompts in 1 – 9.
Lower level groups should write them first as a way
of consolidating the form, while higher level groups
could construct them orally. It is enough for students
to do a few of these, so ask them to complete 4 or 5
of the examples. You might want to provide a few
examples first:

*Once I've managed to find her number, I'm going to
ring my old friend Joan, who I haven't been in touch
with for two years.
As soon as I've finished university, I'm going to travel
the world.*

Workbook

8 Present perfect, page 66

18 Talking Point

Before students do this exercise, they should revise
some of the vocabulary items, expressions,
collocations and structures introduced in this unit.
Put some on the board to help students during their
discussion:

*What I really need / want to do is ...
I might try and ...
As soon as I've ...
Ideally, I'd like to ... but realistically, I'll probably ...
I can see myself ...*

They should also check and translate the expressions
in the Expressions Organiser on page 191.

Look at the Learning Advice on page 149 if you have
not already done so.

Unit 10b
The world of work

Unit overview

Topic

Work and working conditions.

The text

Two casual workers fighting for the right to sick pay
and holiday pay.

Input language

- Vocabulary around working conditions – *sick pay,
  maternity leave, benefits, perks* etc
- Questions to ask about someone's job – *How are
  things at work? What does your job involve?*
- Reporting – *He said he was leaving.*
- Describing a boss – *She's very approachable. He
  spends the whole time sitting at his desk.*
- The future continuous – *I'll be passing your door so
  it's no trouble giving you a lift.*

The language strip

Ask students to find two idioms. Check that they
know what they mean.

Ask them to find as many expressions as they can
which are about working conditions.

1 Working Conditions

Before students open their coursebooks to begin this
unit, check they are familiar with the expression
working conditions. Remind them it was the theme of
a role play on page 139. Ask them what sort of
working conditions are important to them and write
these on the board.

Then get them to open their books and compare the
list on the board with the list in exercise 1. They
should then do the ranking exercise and compare
their results with a partner.

Finish off by seeing if the class can agree on the five
most important aspects of a job.

2 Vocabulary

Students should do this on their own at first, then
check in pairs. Encourage students to use their
dictionaries. Students who finish early should look at
the sentences again and underline important
collocations such as:

*take maternity leave
given a proper contract*

get sick pay
income tax starts at / goes up to
been unfairly treated
work full-time
get three weeks' paid holiday a year
get lots of benefits
a company pension
private health insurance

Remind students to record these in their notebooks.

Answers

1. maternity leave 2. contract 3. sick pay 4. Income tax 5. unfairly treated 6. full-time 7. paid holiday 8. lots of benefits

Vocabulary discussion

This is best done first as a class discussion. Students should then work in pairs to see if any of the sentences might be true for them, or for their parents, at any part of their working lives.

Benefits are what your employer chooses to give you. **Rights** are what you have by law.

Workbook

11 Working conditions, page 67
12 Collocations with *job*, page 67

3 While reading

Get students to give you some examples of *casual work* (fruit picking, shelf-filling in a supermarket, part-time work in a bar).

Check that students understand the three questions. You may need to explain *take their employers to court* (take legal action against their employers) and *implication*. Providing another example may help:

The car factory closing down will have massive implications for the whole community, not just the workers.

Also check that students know the difference between *employer* and *employee* and can pronounce the two clearly.

Then get students to read the text and check the comprehension questions.

Answers

1. Because they were denied benefits normally given to full-time staff.
2. The judge decided the women had the right to the same benefits as the other employees.
3. Other casual workers can fight for benefits from their employers and also they can appeal if they are sacked unfairly.

As an extra exercise, students could add other verb collocations from the text which were not taught in exercise 2. Ask them to find:

Two verbs used with *contract*: offered, refused
Three nouns used with *denied*: holiday pay, sick pay and other benefits

4 Talking Point

Before students discuss the questions in pairs, write some other ways of using the verb *treated* on the board:

I was treated fairly / unfairly / (really) well / like a member of the family / with respect / like a child.

As a follow-up class discussion, try and find the best and worst employer of anyone in the class.

5 Vocabulary work

Students could discuss the questions in small groups before you check them with the class. The collocations exercise will consolidate some items already introduced.

Answers

1. A *full-time worker* works a full week; a *part-time worker* works only part of the week. A *casual worker* is employed only when needed and may be full-time or part-time during that period.
2. People get sacked usually when their work or general behaviour is not good enough for the employer.
3. *Getting sacked* happens for the reason given above. Being *made redundant* is because the employer cannot afford to keep the same number of workers or if there is not enough work.

Useful collocations

1. contract of employment 2. won the right to
3. denied holiday pay 4. refused a proper contract
5. fight for the right to 6. appeal against 7. sacked without reason 8. major breakthrough

6 How are things at work?

There are many typical questions and answers for asking and talking about work. These question and answer pairings are almost as fixed as the *Hello, how are you? Fine thanks* exchange, and students should be encouraged to learn them as whole conversations. In this exercise, there are three answers to match to each question.

Answers

1c 2d 3e 4b 5a

After students have done the matching exercise, get them to cover up the questions, then in pairs take turns trying to remember the questions using the answers to remind them.

Practise the questions and answers around the class. Start by letting students read the expressions from the exercise, and then encourage them to do it from memory. If students are all in work, get them to walk around the class asking and answering questions about their own jobs, using as much of the language from the exercise as possible.

7 Reporting (G39)

Grammar rules for reported speech are often over-simplified and this is explained clearly in the Grammar Commentary on page 186. What is most important is that students are able to recognise that the tense that something is reported in is often different from the original direct speech. After doing the introductory questions, refer students to the Grammar Commentary. Encourage them to be a little more relaxed about the traditional 'rules' for reported speech. Explain that these classroom rules are only partly true.

Then get students to do 1 – 12. When they have finished, they could take turns reading the direct forms in pairs to construct amusing or absurd conversations. For example:

Student 1: I'm leaving for good.
Student 2: I don't care.
Student 1: I've just won some money.
Student 2: It doesn't make any difference.

Answers

1. I'm leaving for good.
2. I don't care.
3. I've just won some money.
4. It doesn't make any difference.
5. I've won £3 million.
6. Money has no effect on me.
7. I've lied to you.
8. You've lied ever since we (first) met.
9. There's only one thing I haven't lied about.
10. What's that?
11. I've always loved you and I've always been true to you.
12. I'll forgive you if you agree to stop spending all your money on lottery tickets.

Grammar discussion

Students try this in pairs then check the answers as a whole class.

Answers

1. And then he said he's emigrating to Australia (if it is still in the future) or
   And then he said he was emigrating ...
2. And then he said it was time to leave if we wanted to catch the train.
3. And then he said he'd crashed his new Mercedes the week before.
4. And then he said I was silly not to have applied for the job.
5. And then he said he'd see me later.
6. And then he said he'd made a terrible mistake.
7. And then he said his house had been on the market for a week.
8. And then he said there must be a mouse in the house.
9. And then he said, *There's no time like the present.*

Workbook

17 Reporting verbs, page 70
18 Passing on messages, page 70

8 What do you do again?

Answers

The jobs are: joiner, street-sweeper, chemist, glassblower, sculptor (Check that students understand the word *joiner*.)

Students can re-use the green sentence starters and ideas from exercise 8 on page 42, in this exercise.

9 What's the job? (T61)

Let students listen to the mini-conversations several times before you discuss the answers. Then play them again and let students read the tapescript on page 175 at the same time.

Then let students practise the mini-conversations with a partner.

Answers

1. chemist 2. joiner 3. street-sweeper

Workbook

13 Two views of work, page 68

10 Role play

Make it clear that students should initially use the questions from exercise 6, but may then go on to ask any other questions they can think of in order to identify the job.

After doing this, students could move on to another partner and repeat the conversation using the **same** job.

To make this into a game, you could limit the amount of time (1 or 2 minutes, depending on level) before students have to move on to another partner. They do this a number of times, writing down the jobs and the name of their different partners as they go. No job names are revealed until the end when points are awarded for correct guesses.

11 The ideal boss

Ask if any students are, or ever have been, bosses. You could also introduce and ask students to record the expressions:

I'm my own boss.
He bosses me around.
He's really quite bossy.

Ask which form of *boss* above is a verb, adjective or noun. You also might like to introduce the expressions:

I'm responsible to ...
I'm responsible for ...

as more formal ways of talking about bosses. Students who work could then tell each other a bit about their positions in their place of work.

Answers

1f 2g 3a 4h 5c 6b 7d 8e

12 Talking Point

Give students a few minutes to look through the 16 sentences in exercise 11 and then tell a partner if any of them could be used about a boss they work (or have worked) for. Then ask larger groups of three or four to discuss the next questions.

Check as a class who students think would be the best boss.

This student could then be put in charge of the cassette for the next activity or given another kind of boss-like responsibility!

Finally, ask students to search through all the pictures in the book and decide who they would most/least like to work for.

13 Boss jokes (T62)

Let students read the jokes while they listen to the tape. Pause after each one to allow students to react. Help with any comprehension problems. Then play the first joke again and ask the class to listen for the stresses and pauses. Quickly write the first joke on the board and mark the stresses and pauses as a class, so that students know what you want them to do. Students can do the other two themselves as you

play the tape as many times as necessary. It is not necessary to do this with all three jokes as it can take a lot of time.

14 The future continuous (G40)

Ask students to look at the first example and tell you which action is already decided (passing the front door) and which action is a new decision or offer (giving a lift). Do the same with the second example. Say these examples for the class to repeat after you, chorally and individually. Then refer them to the Grammar Commentary on page 186. They should then do the matching exercise.

Answers

1e 2f 3a 4b 5d 6c

Grammar in context

This exercise contextualises the earlier expressions. After checking the answers, students should practise saying the mini-conversations with a partner.

Answers

1 – 2,   2 – 1,   3 – 5,   4 – 4,   5 – 6,   6 – 3

Workbook

15 Future continuous, page 69

15 Career plans

Before students do this mingling exercise, revise some of the language from this unit and 10a. Remind students to refer to the Expression Organiser on page 191.

Workbook

19 Writing, page 70

Finally

Assuming you and your students have completed all ten units of *Innovations*, this is the time to review the success of the course and give students advice on how to continue their English learning on their own.

Here are some of the questions you could ask students:

1. How does this course compare with other courses you have studied?
2. Do you feel your spoken English has improved?
3. How has this course changed your ideas about how English is learned?
4. What will you do to continue your learning?

Vocabulary page

Work or job

1. work 2. job 3. work 4. job 5. work 6. job
7. job 8. work

Phrasal verbs with *up*

1. turned 2. hung 3. do 4. come 5. cheer 6. beat
7. bottling 8. put

Hopes and dreams

1b 2a 3g 4f 5c 6e 7d

Working life

unemployed, job, applied, interview, called, got,
salary, manager, promoted, sack, career

Extra workbook exercises

7   Just do it! page 66
10 Collocations, page 67
14 Life is a journey, page 68
16 Phrasal verbs with *up*, page 69

Review: Units 9 and 10

1 Tenses

1. fixed 2. being redecorated 3. be paid 4. they'd
5. I'll be seeing 6. was going to be 7. I've finished
8. I'm going to try 9. been widened

2 Multiple choice

1b 2a 3a 4a 5c 6a 7a 8a

3 Expressions

1b 2e 3a 4d 5c

4 Conversation

1a 2c 3f 4b 5d 6e

5 Collocations

1h 2f 3b 4a 5g 6c 7d 8e

6 Idioms

1g 2e 3a 4f 5b 6c 7h 8d

7 Real English

1e 2c 3a 4f 5d 6b

8 Vocabulary quiz

1. Nothing. 2. A building, part of a town.
3. Not nice.
4. *Flexi-time* means there are no set start and finish
   times to the day; *full-time* means working a full
   working week; *part-time* means working only part
   of a week.
5. No, (s)he is always telling you what to do.
6. No. 7. No. 8. When she's just had a baby.
9. Paternity leave. 10. You get on with her.
11. Complaints, enquiries, phone calls.
12. Deal with them.
13. Canberra, Sofia, Santiago, Cape Town.
14. I can't get a job unless I'm experienced, but I can't
    get experience unless I get a job.
15. If you have been unfairly treated at work or
    unfairly sacked.
16. No, he's just naughty but his parents don't
    punish him at all.
17. The donkey work. 18. The local council.
19. Company pension, company car, private health
    insurance.
20. Sick pay, paid holiday, maternity leave (if you are
    a woman!).